2018

WINGS
OVER
WEXFORD

WINGS OVER WEXFORD

USN AIR STATION WEXFORD 1918-19

LIAM GAUL

To man's first thoughts of flight, from when Icarus flew too near the sun and Leonardo da Vinci's flying machine or ornithopter was a sketch on his drawing board, to the brothers Orville and Wilbur Wright's study of birds in flight at Dayton, Ohio, which led to their first flight in their engine-driven heavier-than-air 'flyer' on 17 December 1903 at Kitty Hawk, North Carolina. Their flight of 120 feet in 12 seconds was just the beginning, for six years later, on 25 July 1909, Louis Blériot, in a propeller-driven aircraft, made the first heavier-than-air crossing of the English Channel. American inventor and aviator, Glenn Hammond Curtiss developed his flying boats in the early years of the twentieth century and these eventually played a leading role in the First World War, combating the enemy U-boats, especially in their brief forays off the south Wexford coast in 1918.

Front cover image: Curtiss H-16 seaplane.
Back cover: 'Tug and Sailing Ships at Wexford Quay', painting by Brian Cleare, 2017. (Brian Cleare)

First published 2017

The History Press Ireland
50 City Quay
Dublin 2
www.thehistorypress.ie

The History Press Ireland is a member of Publishing Ireland, the Irish book publishers' association.

© Liam Gaul, 2017

The right of Liam Gaul to be identified as the Author of this work has been asserted in accordance with the Copyright, Designs and Patents Act 1988.

All rights reserved. No part of this book may be reprinted or reproduced or utilised in any form or by any electronic, mechanical or other means, now known or hereafter invented, including photocopying and recording, or in any information storage or retrieval system, without the permission in writing from the Publishers.

British Library Cataloguing in Publication Data.
A catalogue record for this book is available from the British Library.

ISBN 978 0 7509 8351 8

Typesetting and origination by The History Press
Printed and bound by TJ International

Contents

	About the Author	6
	Acknowledgements	7
	Introduction	9
1	Call to Arms	11
2	War at Sea	17
3	The Yanks Are Coming	25
4	The USN Air Base at Ferrybank	34
5	Wings over Wexford	45
6	The Officers and Crew	58
7	Rosslare Listens	70
8	Wexford 1918	78
9	War Is Over	104
10	Out of Sight	111
11	The Yankee Slip – The Aftermath	122
	Bibliography	131
	Notes	135

About the Author

Liam Gaul is a native of Wexford town and has a keen interest in history, in particular the history of his own place. *Wings over Wexford*, his sixth publication, gives an overview of the war and the part played by the United States Navy while it was based just outside Wexford town in 1918 and 1919. He is a regular contributor to historical journals, periodicals and newspapers and gives lectures to historical societies and local schools. He is a graduate of the University of Limerick, the National University of Ireland (Maynooth) and the Open University. He is currently president of the Wexford Historical Society. Recently, he was awarded a special medallion for his long service to Irish traditional music by Comhaltas Ceoltóirí Éireann. A member of the long-established Wexford Gramophone Society, he presents the occasional gramophone recital at its musical evenings. During the past seven years, Liam has presented a weekly summer radio programme for the Christian Media Trust on South East Radio.

Acknowledgements

I wish to thank the following: Beth Amphlett; Colm Campbell, Riverbank House Hotel; Mrs Maura Cummins, Waterford; Charles and Margot Delaney; Michael Dempsey; Gráinne Doran, county archivist; Laurence Doyle; Dave Fagan, Torquay; Pat Fitzgerald, Cork; Gerry Forde, senior engineer, Environment Department, Wexford County Council; Mary Gallagher; Margaret Gilhooley, Ely Hospital; Jarlath Glynn; Tomás Hayes; Ken Hemmingway; Jack Higginbotham; Tony Kearns, aviation historian; Michael Kelly; Captain Seán McCarthy, press officer, Irish Air Corps, Baldonnell Airport; Denise O'Connor-Murphy; Jack O'Leary, maritime historian; Anne O'Neill, An Post, Irish Stamps, GPO, Dublin; Mary O'Rourke, Ferrybank Motors; Angela Parle, Library Service; Frank Pelly; Joan Rockley; Seamus and Joe Seery; the staff of Wexford County Library; Bob Thomas, USA; Airman Michael J. Whelan, Irish Air Corps; and the Friday Historians – Aidan, Billy, Ken, Nicky, Seamus and Tom. To my publisher, Ronan Colgan and The History Press Ireland.

Finally, my sincere thanks to my wife and family for their interest, support and patience.

Photographic credits: Jim Billington; Ann Borg; Brian Cleare; Lisa Crunk, CA photo archivist, Naval History & Heritage Command, Washington; Charles Delaney; Nicholas Furlong; Jim Gaul, Cobh, Co. Cork; Liam Gaul; Billy Kelly, Kelly's Resort Hotel, Rosslare; John Hayes; Irish Air Corps, Baldonnell; Michael Kavanagh; Marc Levitt, archivist, National Aviation Museum, Pensacola, FL; Dermot McCarthy; Veronica Murphy, USA; the

National Library of Ireland; Cathleen Noland, USA; James and Sylvia O'Connor; Brian O'Hagan; Niall Reck; Padge Reck; Sr Grace Redmond, Presentation Convent, Wexford; Nicky Rossiter; An Canónach Séamus S. de Vál SP; Matt Wheeler, Irish Agricultural Museum Archive, Johnstown Castle; Sheila Wilmot, Duncannon, Co. Wexford.

South-east coastal map of County Wexford. (L. Gaul)

Introduction

The year 2018 marks the centenary of the United States Naval Air Base being established at Tincone, Ferrybank North,[1] across the River Slaney from the town of Wexford in the south-east corner of Ireland. Although the base was just in operation for the final few months of the First World War (1914–18), it had a profound effect on the German submarine activity in St George's Channel and the Irish Sea. Several U-boats were spotted and bombed by the seaplanes guarding the busy shipping lane, ensuring safe passage for both British naval vessels and merchant ships plying the waters between Ireland and England.

By 1919, all American personnel had vacated the air base and returned home to the USA. All buildings on the site were dismantled and sold off at auction, and soon nature had reclaimed the land and the area became a green field site once again. In the ensuing decades, the USN Air Base and its wartime activities were lost in the mists of time and memory, especially after the termination of British rule in Ireland and the emergence of a new Ireland.

Ely House and Bann-a-boo House had played an important role during the American occupation of the area, serving as the residences of the US naval officers and the centre of all planning activities during those months. Ely House has disappeared and has been replaced by Ely Hospital, while Bann-a-boo House has taken on a new form as a hotel, which incorporates some of the original building. The main frontage of the former USN Air Base is now occupied by a very successful garage and car dealership.

Many Wexford residents are totally unaware of the existence of the air base in the area a century ago but renowned singer and author, Nellie Walsh, recalled seaplanes flying over Wexford in the opening chapter of her book, *Tuppences Were for Sundays*:[2] 'Recently during a committee meeting of the Wexford Historical Society of which I have been a member since its inception in 1944, somebody mentioned being questioned about World War One and Wexford's connection with it.' Nellie goes on to say there was a laugh around the table when she described the beautiful flying boats or seaplanes landing in the harbour waters. At that time, the present Wexford Bridge did not exist and the only crossing was further up the river at Carcur. According to Nellie, the other committee members looked at her in dismay and disbelief. She went on to say, 'I was talking of a completely lost life and maybe we should hand on our memories.'[3]

What was life like in Wexford and its environs at that time and what effects did the war have on the people of the area? With the shortage of food and clothing and work in the town, was there also a decline in business? Industrial unrest brought strikes for better wages and working conditions in the town's few industries. Many Wexford men answered the call issued by John Edward Redmond MP to take up arms and enlist in the British Army to fight in Belgium and France, with grave consequences for themselves and the families they left behind. Wexford soldiers lie in unmarked graves on the Continent, with their names engraved in stone on a distant war memorial. Near the end of the war, how did the American aviators and crews interact with the local people and were friendships forged with the new arrivals on our quiet shore?

I will endeavour to record for posterity this long-forgotten era in Wexford's past and answer the questions raised about the Americans who came to Wexford to set up and operate an air base at Ferrybank. During that year, there were wings over Wexford.

1

Call to Arms

Disagreements in Europe over territory and boundaries, among other issues, came to a head with the assassination of Archduke Ferdinand of Austria[1] in Sarajevo at the hands of Gavrilo Princip, a Serbian nationalist, on 28 June 1914. Princip had ties to the secretive military group known as the Black Hand.[2] This assassination propelled the major European military powers towards war. Exactly one month later, the First World War had begun. In 1915, the British passenger liner the RMS *Lusitania* was sunk by a German submarine, killing 128 Americans and further heightening tensions. By the end of 1915, Austria-Hungary, Bulgaria, Germany and the Ottoman Empire were battling the Allied Powers of Britain, France, Russia, Italy, Belgium, Serbia, Montenegro and Japan.

Many Americans were not in favour of their country entering the war and wanted to remain neutral. The desire for neutrality was strong among Americans of Irish, German, and Swedish descent, as well as among Church leaders and women. The American people increasingly came to see the German Empire as the villain after news of atrocities in Belgium in 1914. President Woodrow Wilson[3] made all the key decisions and kept the economy on a peacetime basis, while giving large-scale loans to Britain and France. To avoid being seen to make any military threat, President Wilson made only minimal preparations for war and kept the American Army on its small peacetime basis as more and more demands were being made to prepare for war. The president did enlarge the United States Navy.

After two and a half years of efforts by President Wilson to keep the United States neutral, the US entered the war on 6 April 1917. They joined their allies, Britain, France and Russia, to fight in the First World War. Under the command of Major General John J. Pershing,[4] more than 2 million American soldiers fought on the battlefields of France.

In early 1917, Germany had decided to resume all-out submarine warfare on every commercial ship headed towards Britain, in the knowledge that this decision would almost certainly mean war with the United States. President Wilson asked Congress to vote on the US entering an all-out war that would make the world a safer and more democratic place. The United States Congress voted to declare war on Germany on 6 April 1917. On 7 December 1917, the US declared war on the Austro-Hungarian Empire.

With the entry of the United States into the First World War, Europe witnessed the arrival of US forces in a bid to assist the Allied cause. The German U-boats were causing havoc in the English Channel. In an effort to halt the huge losses, the British Admiralty requested that the United States establish Naval Air Stations in Ireland and Britain.

A critical indirect strategy used by both sides was the blockade. The British Royal Navy successfully stopped the shipment of most war supplies and food to Germany. Neutral American ships that tried to trade with Germany were seized or turned back by the Royal Navy, who deemed such trade to be in direct conflict with the Allies' war efforts. Germany and the Central Powers, its allies, controlled extensive farmlands and raw materials. The blockade was eventually successful as Germany and Austria-Hungary had depleted their agricultural production by enlisting so many farmers into their armies. By 1918, German cities were on the verge of starvation; the front-line soldiers were on short rations and were running out of essential supplies. The German war effort seemed to be winding down and would eventually grind to a halt.

The Germans also considered a blockade. Admiral Alfred von Tirpitz,[5] the man who built the German fleet and a key advisor to the Kaiser Wilhelm II,[6] maintained that Germany would play the same game as Britain and destroy every ship that tried to break the blockade. Although unable to challenge the more powerful Royal Navy on the surface, Tirpitz vowed to scare off all merchant and passenger ships en route to Britain. He believed that since the island of Britain depended on imports of food, raw materials and manufactured goods, scaring off a substantial number of the ships would effectively undercut its long-term ability to maintain an army on the Western Front. Germany had only nine long-range U-boats at the start of the war, but it had ample shipyard capacity to build the hundreds needed. However, the United States demanded that Germany respect the international agreements regarding the 'freedom of the seas',[7] which protected neutral American ships on the high seas from seizure or sinking by either of the warring sides. The

Americans insisted that the drowning of innocent civilians was barbaric and grounds for a declaration of war.

The British frequently violated America's neutral rights by seizing ships. President Wilson's top advisor, Colonel Edward M. House,[8] commented that, 'The British have gone as far as they possibly could in violating neutral rights, though they have done it in the most courteous way.' When President Wilson protested British violations of American neutrality, the British backed down.

German submarines torpedoed ships without warning, causing sailors and passengers to drown. Berlin explained that submarines were so vulnerable that they dared not surface near merchant ships that might be carrying guns and that were too small to rescue submarine crews. Britain armed most of its merchant ships with medium-calibre guns that could sink a submarine, making above-water attacks too risky. In February 1915, the United States warned Germany about the misuse of submarines. On 22 April, the German Imperial Embassy warned US citizens about boarding vessels to Great Britain, which would risk German attack. On 7 May, Germany torpedoed the British passenger liner RMS *Lusitania*, sinking her. This act of aggression caused the loss of 1,198 civilian lives, including 128 Americans. President Wilson issued a warning to Germany that it would face 'strict accountability' if it sank more neutral US passenger ships. Berlin acquiesced, ordering its submarines to avoid passenger ships.

By January 1917, however, Field Marshal Paul von Hindenburg[9] and General Erich Ludendorff[10] decided that an unrestricted submarine blockade was the only way to break the stalemate on the Western Front. They demanded that Kaiser Wilhelm order unrestricted submarine warfare be resumed. Germany knew this decision meant war with the United States, but they gambled that they could win before America's potential strength could be mobilised. However, they overestimated how many ships they could sink and thus the extent to which Britain would be weakened, and they did not foresee that convoys could and would be used to defeat their efforts. They believed that the United States was so weak militarily that it could not be a factor on the Western Front for more than a year. The civilian government in Berlin objected, but the kaiser sided with his military. Germany formally surrendered on 11 November 1918 and all nations agreed to stop fighting while the terms of peace were negotiated.

The foundation of the USN Air Stations in Ireland and England, although operational for just a few short months, played an important role in undermining the dominance of the U-boats in the seas around both countries.

A 'call to arms' war poster.

The station at Wexford was very active and carried out many missions in search of the submarines, which operated with devastating effect in and around Tuskar Rock Lighthouse and up along the Irish and English coastlines. The presence of the American aviators was reassuring for ship owners on the coast who had been concerned about the safety of their vessels, their cargoes and especially the crews of their ships.

In 1912, John Edward Redmond MP, leader of the Irish Parliamentary Party, was negotiating the introduction of what was to be the Third Home Rule Bill with the British Prime Minister and Liberal Party leader, Herbert Henry Asquith (1852–1928), which eventually reached the statute books on 18 September 1914. The Third Home Rule Bill had passed the House of Commons, albeit with a small majority, but was totally rejected by the House of Lords. The bill was voted on and defeated by the House of Lords again in 1913.

Dublin-born Sir Edward Carson (1854–1935), together with the Irish Unionist Party, strongly opposed the Home Rule Bill and in 1912 more than 500,000 people signed the Ulster Covenant against the passing of such

CALL TO ARMS

a bill. To ensure that this bill was not passed and brought into law, an Ulster Volunteer Force was formed to oppose such a measure by force, if necessary.

The Home Rule Bill was passed again by the House of Commons in May 1914, when the government overrode the opposition by the House of Lords by implementing the provisions of the Parliament Act of 1911. The bill would have meant the creation of a two-chamber Irish parliament consisting of a 164-seat House of Commons and a 40-seat Senate. Ireland would retain the right to elect Members of Parliament to sit in Westminster. The bill was sent for Royal Assent.[11] The king signed the Home Rule Bill at noon on Friday, 18 September, together with an Act suspending the Home Rule Bill from coming into effect, with all further parliamentary debate postponed until the war ended.

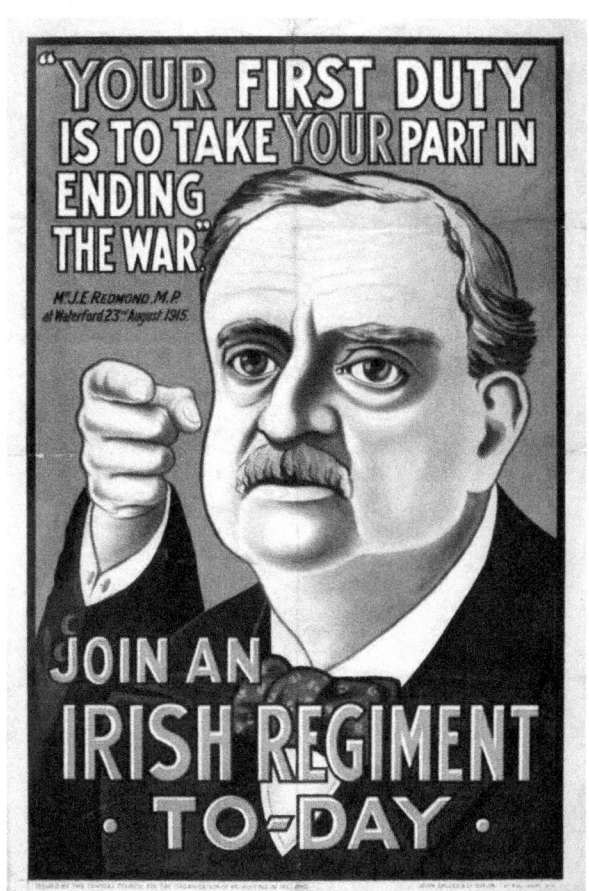

John Edward Redmond MP – war poster. (National Library of Ireland)

15

On his return home to Ireland on the Sunday morning, Redmond set out for his home at Aughavanagh, Co. Wicklow. He stopped his car at Woodenbridge in the Vale of Avoca, where he encountered an assembly of the East Wicklow Volunteers. Present were the two Wicklow MPs and Colonel Maurice Moore, Inspector-General of the Volunteers. John Redmond, in a short, impromptu address to the group, outlined their duty:

> to go on drilling and to account yourselves as men, not only in Ireland itself, but wherever the firing-line extends, in defence of freedom and of religion in this war where it would be a disgrace forever to Ireland, and a reproach to her manhood if young Irishmen were to stay at home to defend the island's shores from an unlikely invasion.

Redmond's Woodenbridge speech became better known than his manifesto on this subject.[12] Redmond pledged the Irish Volunteers to the defence of Ireland and called on Irish men to enlist in the army.

A clarion call had been sounded to participate in a war that would supposedly be finished by Christmas.

2

War at Sea

The Entente Powers – France, Britain and Russia – had a distinct advantage in the struggle to be the victors of the Great War: they had control of the seas, which gave them access to the entire globe, whereas Germany and Austria-Hungary were restricted to the areas they controlled. The British high command were convinced that the only way to end the war was to annihilate the German Army in a head-on confrontation. This decision condemned 60,000 men to certain death or maiming during the autumn in the Battle of Loos.

At sea, the battle fleets spent most of their time tied up in harbour, with occasional engagements like the Battle of Jutland fought mainly at a distance, without serious risks. The Battle of Jutland lasted from 31 May to 1 June 1916 and involved 250 ships and 100,000 men. It was the only major naval engagement of the First World War. The British Grand Fleet had a greater number of ships than the German High Sea Fleet, with 37 heavy warships and 113 lighter support ships versus the Germans' 27 heavy warships and 72 support ships. The British Intelligence Service had also broken the German signalling codes.

The Battle of Jutland began at 4.48 p.m. on 31 May, when the scouting forces of vice admirals David Beatty and Franz von Hipper[1] began a running artillery duel at a range of 15,000 yards in the Skagerrak (Jutland), just off Denmark's North Sea coast. Hipper's battleships took a barrage of severe shelling, but they survived, thanks to their superior honeycomb hull construction. Vice Admiral Beatty lost three battleships due to fires in the gun turrets started by incoming shells reaching the powder magazines. Beatty turned his ships north and lured the German ships on to the Grand Fleet.

At 7.15 p.m., the second phase of the battle started. Admiral John Jellicoe,[2] by executing a 90-degree wheel-to-port, brought his ships into a single battle line, thus gaining the advantage of the fading evening light. Admiral Jellicoe cut the German fleet off from its home base and he twice crossed the High Seas Fleet. The German commander Admiral Reinhard Scheer's[3] ships took over seventy direct hits while his ships scored just twenty against the British Grand Fleet. This would have meant complete annihilation for Scheer's fleet, were it not for his three brilliant 180-degree turns away from the danger. By darkness at 10.00 p.m., the British has lost 6,784 men and 111,000 tons of shipping, with German losses amounting to 3,058 men and 62,000 tons.

On the morning of 1 June, Admiral Jellicoe's fleet stood off Wilhelmshaven with his twenty-four untouched dreadnoughts and battlecruisers. Sheer kept his ten battle-ready heavy fighting ships in port. The German High Seas Fleet had been sent home and would only be put to sea three more times on minor missions. Admiral Scheer avoided future surface encounters with the Grand Fleet due to its great material superiority and instead demanded the defeat of Britain's economic life by concentrating on the use of U-boats in the war at sea.[4]

The submarine was developed from an earlier invention by John Holland (1841–1914), from Liscannor, Co. Clare. It was brought into extensive use by Germany in the First World War in the battle for supremacy and control of the conflict at sea. This 'tin fish' created havoc for ships off the Wexford coast, destroying thousands of tons of ships and the crews who manned those vessels. The same John Holland, a member of the Irish Christian Brothers, taught science at the Christian Brothers School in Enniscorthy, Co. Wexford, prior to emigrating to the United States in 1872. It was there that he developed his submarine, but he died in 1914 without ever witnessing the result of his genius.[5]

Two major sea disasters happened during the First World War, namely the sinking of the RMS *Lusitania* on Friday, 7 May 1915 and the *Leinster* on Thursday, 10 October 1918, with the loss of many lives.

The *Lusitania*, dubbed the 'Greyhound of the Seas', made her maiden voyage from Liverpool to New York in September 1907, powered by her 68,000-horsepower engines. The ship took the Blue Ribbon for the fastest crossing of the Atlantic. This leviathan of the seas was secretly financed by the British Admiralty and was built to specifications set by the Admiralty. In the event of war, the ship would be consigned to government service. In 1913, as war was becoming ever more likely, the giant vessel was fitted for war service. Ammunition magazines and gun mounts were installed, with the mounts concealed under the main deck timbers in readiness for the addition of guns.

'The Sinking of the *Leinster*' by Brian Cleare. (Dominic Carroll)

Two years later, on Saturday, 7 May 1915, the *Lusitania* sailed from New York, bound for Liverpool. Practically all of the ship's hidden cargo consisted of munitions and contraband destined for Britain's war effort, unknown to the passengers on board. It is probable the Germans were aware of the secret cargo being carried by the ship. The luxurious liner could travel so fast that there may have been a certain confidence that she could outrun any submarine with ease. The fear of being attacked by a submarine had reduced the number of passengers on board to half the ship's usual capacity on that ill-fated voyage. It was at 2.10 p.m. on the afternoon of Friday, 7 May, as the liner neared the Old Head of Kinsale, that a torpedo fired by the German submarine, SM-U20, crashed into the ship's side.

A mysterious second explosion ripped the liner apart. The ship listed badly as chaos reigned. Lifeboats smashed into passengers crowded on deck. So sudden was the attack and the ensuing explosions that many of the passengers never had a chance. The giant ship slipped beneath the waves, resulting in the deaths of 1,119 of the 1,924 passengers on board. Amongst the dead were 114 Americans, including Alfred Vanderbilt, one of the richest men in the world, and Carl Frohman, the playwright. Both Vanderbilt and Frohman went to the ship's nursery and tied life jackets to the Moses baskets containing small babies in an attempt to save their lives and to prevent them from going down with the ship. The baskets were carried off by the rising water, but none of the infants survived.

The former captain of the *Lusitania*, Captain Daniel Dow, had retired from his position due to stress and had been replaced with a new commander, Captain William Thomas Turner, who was in command of the ship on this fatal voyage.

The *Lusitania* sank within eighteen minutes. At the time, this sinking was considered senseless slaughter as the *Lusitania* was a non-military passenger ship. The horrific actions of the SM-U20 submarine and its commander Kapitänleutnant Walther Schwieger aided Britain's propaganda efforts.[6] Although identified as a passenger liner by Schwieger, he ordered his crew to fire one torpedo which struck the ship just below the bridge. Following the outrage against the sinking, the German kaiser was forced to apologise for this maritime tragedy, but Captain Schwieger was not reprimanded for his actions.

The SM-U20 submarine was one of the deadliest naval weapons developed by Imperial Germany. Built by Kaiserliche Werft Marine in Danzig, this submarine was launched in 1912. It measured 210 feet in length, 20 feet in width and 23 feet from top to bottom and it had a crew of thirty-one men and four officers. Its speed was rated at 15 knots (28 kilometres per hour)

Lusitania centenary postage stamp. (An Post)

Leinster centenary postage stamp. (An Post)

and it could achieve depths of about 164 feet. The SM-U20 could launch the six torpedoes on board from two torpedo tubes, fore and aft. The craft also had a quick-loading cannon and a Hotchkiss machine gun. During the First World War, the SM-U20 was assigned operations patrolling the waters around the British Isles. A total of thirty-six ships were sent to the bottom of the sea by Captain Schwieger before his vessel accidentally ran aground near the Danish coast in 1916. The officers and crew abandoned ship and the next day scuttled the submarine by exploding its torpedoes in an effort to keep it out of enemy hands.

The torpedoing of the Irish mail-boat *Leinster* on Thursday morning, 10 October 1918, caused the deaths of several hundred passengers and provoked utter horror throughout the civilised world, and Ireland in particular, as most of the victims were Irish. The ill-fated ship was built for speed and time and again she had escaped the attacks of the U-boat commanders. She now lies at the bottom of the sea, with the vast majority of her human freight.

The commander of the *Leinster*, Captain Birch, was an extremely capable seaman. His ship was the most popular boat in the cross-channel service and its accommodation was always filled to capacity. The *Leinster* left Kingstown (Dún Laoghaire) pier on Thursday morning at the usual time, with the usual heavy complement of mail and passengers, and proceeded on its journey for about one hour. The ship was then struck on the port bow by a torpedo, with a second torpedo following some three or four minutes later. The torpedoes struck the ship almost amidships, practically splitting her into two parts. She sank within ten minutes of being struck for the second time.

It is believed that the submarine fired three torpedoes, with the first one missing the *Leinster*, passing some yards in front of the bow of the vessel. Captain Birch realised the danger immediately and altered course, swinging his ship away to starboard, but the manoeuvre could not be carried out in time to avoid the second torpedo. Many people were killed in their berths and others were so badly injured that they could not make their way up on deck.

While the lifeboats were being lowered and the passengers were crowding into them, the second torpedo crashed into the ship, penetrating the engine room, and exploded, blowing the ship into two parts. The explosion killed a number of the passengers and crew and practically demolished the post office sorting rooms, killing the sorting staff. Of a staff of twenty-two, only one post office worker survived. The explosion threw that one post office worker out of the ship, into the sea. The German submarine partly surfaced, saw that the mail-boat had been destroyed, submerged and sped away.

A wireless SOS was sent out after the first torpedo struck the ship and the message was picked up by a number of ships in the Channel, of both the Mercantile Marine and the Royal Navy. It was over an hour before the first of the rescue ships arrived at the scene of the disaster. In total 190 people, who had managed to save themselves by clinging onto upturned boats and rafts, were picked up. Over 150 bodies were recovered that day and for days afterwards the corpses of many more of the victims were found floating in the sea. Terrible scenes were witnessed as the bodies were landed at Kingstown pier, where anxious relatives eagerly awaited the arrival of the survivors, hoping their loved ones would be among them. Amongst the victims were honeymooning couples and newly-weds who had parted from their beloveds when the vessel departed and were left separated forever.

Two of the casualties on the Royal Mail steamer were prominent businessmen and public figures: Mr John S. Hearn, JP, from New Ross and Mr Thomas L. Esmonde, of Kilgibbon, Enniscorthy. John Hearn was known as a gentleman of good personality with great business capabilities. He was prominently associated with the Star Ironworks in Wexford and was also an employer in New Ross. He was a member of the Urban Council and represented his district on Wexford County Council. His only son was an officer in the Army Training School. Mr Thomas L. Esmonde was chairman

WAR AT SEA

of the board of the Wexford Bacon Factory and was founder of the Farmers' Union and chairman of the County Committee of Agriculture.

Other victims from County Wexford included Mrs Elizabeth Clarke from Blackwater, who was returning home from Liverpool following a visit to her sister. She was buried in Blackwater. Lieutenant Joseph A. Furlong also died. He was the son of Michael Furlong, St Louis, Missouri, and formerly of Lough, Duncormick. Lieutenant Furlong was returning to his duty in the USA Medical Reserve, after having visited his father's home. The lieutenant was buried in the cemetery at Carrick-on-Bannow.

On Saturday, 19 October 1918, the *Free Press* reported the disaster as follows:

A Wexford town man, Mr. James Billington, South Main Street, was among the survivors. Mr Billington is a member of the Harbour Board. James Billington described the scene as one he will never forget when he witnessed almost five hundred people struggling in the water some clinging to rafts and others kept afloat by their lifebelts. 'Nearly one hundred of the swimmers tried to clamber into our boat which was already overcrowded and half-filled with water. We had great difficulty getting the women and children aboard but the sailors gave assistance in this effort. We were landed at Kingstown where we were well looked after'. Mr. Billington, who had suffered from shock for days afterwards paid a tribute to the manner in which the survivors were treated. When asked by the reporter from the Free Press if he had seen any other Wexfordmen

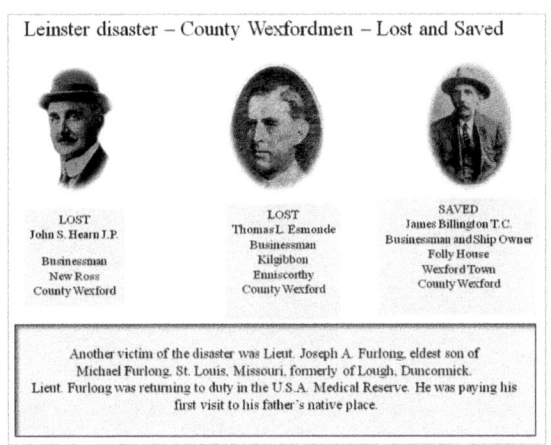

Leinster – disaster – LOST and SAVED. (L. Gaul)

aboard the doomed ship he said: 'He had seen Mr T.L. Esmonde reading in the saloon before the disaster occurred but did not see him again afterwards.'

Another survivor, John Lacey, a native of Wexford, one of the deck hands of the *Leinster* had finished his work and gone below decks and was in his berth when the first explosion took place and scrambling, unhurt, from a mass of splinters, made his way on deck. Passengers were running to and fro in total confusion. His boat station was No. 4 on the starboard side aft and while the boat was still in the davits it was full of passengers. The boat was lowered to the water safely. Lacey said: 'I saw Captain Birch on the bridge and another officer, and, I think, a sailor'. At the second strike by a torpedo Lacey and some of his mates were flung from the top deck some 40 feet of a drop into the sea. He got into the lifeboat and manned one of the oars and rowed for the shore.[7]

The war at sea was a devastating one for sailors and ships from both sides, mainly due to the submarines and their deadly missiles. The establishment of the USN Air Station at Ferrybank, Wexford, helped in no uncertain manner to eradicate the threat to shipping in that final year of war.

3

The Yanks Are Coming

The Royal Navy had a base at Queenstown, County Cork (later named Cobh). This location was appropriate for such a base as it is a spacious natural harbour with ample room for many warships. It was thought of as a pleasant place to be based because it was removed from the naval action at sea. With the entry into the war of the dreaded German submarine, everything would change at Queenstown. At that time, the only British naval vessels in the harbour were a couple of torpedo boats and eight old cruisers used for training.

The U-boats, or submarines, first appeared in the Irish Sea in early January 1915 and within days showed their effectiveness in sinking both merchant and naval vessels, with great losses of ships and their crews. By February, Germany declared that the seas around Britain and Ireland were in a war zone and ships would be targeted, which was a cause of great concern to the British Admiralty at that time.

After the torpedo attack on the passenger liner *Lusitania* in May 1915, which resulted in hundreds of lives being lost, most of them American, the United States entered the war and joined with the Allies in 1917. The German U-boats were active along the shipping lanes close to the coastline of Ireland, rather than the open seas of the North Atlantic, and were controlling the Western Approaches to Great Britain, as well as the Northern and Southern Approaches. With these concentrated attacks on shipping carrying supplies of food and other goods for everyday survival, it became very clear that Britain and its population would starve. With such great losses, it was essential that the U-boat threat be stopped immediately.

An anti-submarine group was set up in December 1916 with the sole object of countering and eventually defeating the menace of the U-boat attacks. Destroyers, air patrols and convoys of warships were to be deployed around the coastlines in this massive effort to combat the enemy. The base at Queenstown would soon become an important part of these new tactics, with its commander Admiral Lewis Bayly assuming the role of Commander-in-Chief of the Western Approaches. In early 1917, the Admiralty carried out surveys throughout Ireland to locate the most appropriate areas, both north and south, to establish air bases to launch air patrols. The main aircraft to be employed were flying boats of the Royal Naval Air Service (RNAS), which required sheltered waters, enabling the flying boats to operate in varying wind conditions. The Admiralty finally selected four main locations: Whiddy Island in Bantry Bay, County Cork; Lough Foyle in County Donegal; Ferrybank, close to Wexford town; and Aghada, County Cork, which was to be the principal site. A site at the Dublin docklands was one of the original proposals for the assembly of the aircraft and the training of pilots, but Aghada was the

Admiral Lewis Bayly, Royal Navy.

final selection and would be the headquarters for all flying boat activities, including for the other Irish air stations.

On 6 April 1917, following the declaration of war by America, an advance guard of six destroyers from the US Atlantic Naval Fleet, led by Commander Joseph Taussig of the USS *Wadsworth*, set out for Cork Harbour. They arrived on 4 May 1917. On the arrival of the fleet, Commander Taussig was asked when his destroyers would be ready for action. He is reported to have replied, 'We are ready now, sir.'[1]

Admiral Bayly gave Taussig just four days to prepare. According to Taussig's diary entries, by 7 May 1917, a naval strategy had been worked out.

The destroyers, British and American, were to work in seven pairs for the short term. Taussig's fleet was to replace the larger British naval destroyers, which were to be sent back to the British base at Plymouth in the English Channel.

The destroyers were to be made to work six days at sea. Ships chasing a submarine on the sixth day, with two thirds of their fuel gone, were to stop chasing their folly and come home. Shelter was to be taken in bad weather. When shipwrecked crews were picked up, they had to be brought directly into the harbour. As German submarines were returning to torpedoed and floating steamers to get metal from them, destroyers were encouraged to wait and approach them with the sun at their back. If they met what appeared to be a valuable ship in dangerous waters, they were to escort her. If an SOS call was received and they thought they could be in time to help, they were to go and assist the ship, but as a rule, they were not to go over 50 miles from their area. Destroyers were to be careful not to ram boats to sink them as there had been cases of them being left with bombs in them, ready to explode when struck.

Senior officers of destroyers were to give the necessary orders with regard to what speed to cruise at and orders for zig-zagging; they knew the capabilities of their ships best.

When escorting, it had been found that the best method, as a rule, was to cross from bow to bow, the ideal distance from the ship being about 1,000 yards. However, this depended on a myriad of factors, including sea conditions and visibility.

Reports of proceedings were not required on arrival in harbour except for some special reason, such as signalling for preparing for attacking submarines and rescuing survivors.

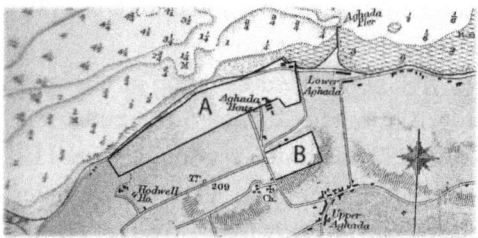

Map of Aghada, showing sites of USN Air Base.

Much confidence was placed in the strategic mind of Commander Taussig. Like his father before him, Joseph was a well-known figure, known to have exceptional ability as a naval officer.

Both the British and US governments combined their efforts in a campaign for the duration of the war, with Admiral Bayly[2] assuming overall command of operations. Cork Harbour soon became crowded with forty-seven US Navy destroyers, seven British sloops, eight minesweeper sloops, nine Q-ships[3] and trawlers, drifters and motor launches.

The flagship of the US fleet, USS *Melville*, carrying Admiral William Sims,[4] commander of the American Forces, also arrived in Cork Harbour, making it one of the most important naval bases in the world.

Admiral William Simms, US Navy.

Even though the American fleet was ready to engage in war, the Naval Aviation Command was totally unprepared for such deployment in a war zone. The USN Command was comprised of only 48 officers and 239 enlisted men. Its one air station was located at Pensacola in Florida, with fifty-four training aircraft, one free balloon and one kite balloon. Upon entering the First World War, America established twenty-four air stations in Europe, including sixteen in France, two in England, two in Italy and four in Ireland, including Ferrybank in Wexford.

Commander Frank R. McCrary assumed overall command of all the US Naval Stations in Ireland on 14 February 1918 and was based at Aghada, where he remained in this capacity for the duration of the war. Lieutenant Commander Paul J. Peyton was the commander of the Aghada base itself. All aircraft assembly and repair for Ireland was carried out at this station; the seaplanes arrived in packing cases from the US. Following assembly, the seaplanes were dispatched to their designated air stations. All aircrew were also trained at this Cork location. Seaplanes from Aghada patrolled the skies from Cape Clear and into the English Channel and also linked with the sea area covered by the Ferrybank patrol from Ferrybank, Wexford. The seaplanes were mainly flown at 1,000 feet on patrol or involved in escort duty.

During the period that the Curtiss H-16s were flying out from Aghada, Ensign M.J. Dwyer, Senior Flying Officer G.L. Compo, one observer, one engineer and one radio officer broke an existing flying time record by remaining airborne while on patrol for 9 hours and 37 minutes.

As the war came to an end, there were 48 officers and 1,398 men at Aghada. There had been 155 flying missions, over 245 hours of flying time and an overall distance covered of 11,568 miles. The seaplanes escorted six convoys and sixty-four patrols.[5]

The seaplanes flown by the aviators based at the US Naval Air Stations in Ireland were Curtiss H-16s developed by the American aviation pioneer and founder of the US aircraft industry, Glenn Hammond Curtiss (1878–1930). He began his career as a builder of racing bicycles and graduated to the manufacture of motorcycles. He began to manufacture aircraft engines in 1904 and in 1908 joined the Aerial Experiment Association founded by Alexander Graham Bell to build flying machines. Eventually his very important contribution to the building and design of aircraft led to the Curtiss Aeroplane and Motor Company being set up. This company built aircraft for the US Army and Navy and prior to the outbreak of WWI his work developing seaplanes brought great advances in naval aviation.

USN personnel at Queenstown, Co. Cork. (Naval History and Heritage Command (NHHC))

The Curtiss factory built a total of sixty-eight 'Large Americas', which became the H-12 aircraft. This was the only American-designed and American-built plane that saw combat in the First World War. The US Navy commissioned Glenn Curtiss to design and build a long-range four-engine flying boat capable of carrying a crew of five in 1917. This aircraft developed into what became known as the NC-4. An experienced pilot, Curtiss trained the navy's first pilots and built their first aircraft. In America, Glenn Hammond Curtiss is known as the 'Father of Naval Aviation'.[6]

The Curtiss H series of seaplanes was at its peak with the introduction of the Model H-16. This model had a longer wingspan, giving much better control of the airplane, and the hull was strengthened, resulting in overall larger dimensions. This H-16 carried a four-man crew. The plane was powered by two Liberty or Rolls-Royce Eagle V12 360 horsepower engines.

Glenn Hammond Curtiss, inventor and aviator.

The wingspan measured 92.71 feet and the plane was 46.5 feet long and 16.5 feet in height. Its gross weight was 10,650lbs. Maximum speed was 85mph, with a flight duration of six hours. It was armed with four .303 Lewis guns on flexible mounts and carried four 100lb or two 230lb bombs beneath the wings.

The crew of a H-16 consisted of two pilots and two machine-gunners. The pilots were seated in a partially enclosed cockpit flight deck at the front end of the fuselage. One of the gunners sat in the forwardmost open-air cockpit at the front of the fuselage. The second gunner manned a dorsal gun position amidships aft of the wing assemblies. The wings were mounted high on the fuselage.

A Curtiss H-16 at Queenstown, Co. Cork.

Commander Frank R. McCrary. (Naval History and Heritage Command (NHHC))

The H-16 retained the earlier Curtiss boat-like hull, which gave the aircraft the ability to land on water. The seaplane aspect of the Curtis H-16 was a great advantage, enabling the plane to land and take off from the water, qualities which served it very well when hunting down enemy surface ships or submarines, or locating 'downed' airmen or seamen. Seaplanes played an important role during the war.[7]

Today, the large concrete apron built by the US Navy has been used by the Lower Aghada Tennis and Sailing Club as a playing area, the 'Yankee' road built by the Americans is an important part of the parish infrastructure and the large slipway for launching the seaplanes is still there. This is the legacy of a forgotten era which began a century ago when the 'Yanks' arrived in Ireland.[8]

Wings of the USN Aviation Corps. (USN Souvenir Book)

4

The USN Air Base at Ferrybank

Following the United States' entry into the First World War, in co-operation with the British Admiralty, five United States Air Stations were in operation in Ireland at Queenstown, Whiddy Island, Lough Foyle and Ferrybank, Wexford and the fifth, a kite balloon station, was located at Berehaven in West Cork. Two other air stations were operating in England from Killingholme in Lincolnshire[1] and Eastleigh in Hampshire.[2] Construction of all the stations commenced in March 1918 under the supervision of US Navy civil engineers. The base at Ferrybank was built by British, Irish and US naval forces and civilians.

Construction of the base at Ferrybank, Wexford, had been started by the British Admiralty in the early weeks of 1918, before the US Naval Air Station was taken over by the US Navy. Contract civilian labour was used to lay the roads and the concrete hangar foundations, drainage systems, reservoir and reserve water tanks, aprons and the slipway. The field which would eventually be the location of the aircraft hangars was drained, but this initial work certainly did not give the impression that an air station would ever be completed at Ferrybank.

During the initial building, there were several industrial disputes which were eventually resolved. There was also a fracas between two of the English foremen, which resulted in a court hearing.[3] The civilians were also involved in the erection of the first aircraft hangar, but due to some grievance a general strike was called, resulting in a work stoppage. With the departure of the civilian workforce from the site, the naval personnel took on the unfinished work, which proceeded at a rapid rate. The civilian crew, realising their mistake, requested that they be allowed to resume work under the old conditions.

Had more navy men been available, contract labour would have been dispensed with and the entire naval station completed in a much shorter time.

On 25 February that same year, the first United States Naval Forces arrived at the site from Queenstown under the command of Officer Charles A. Rogers. There were eight men, including Gunner Rogers. They spent their first week doing a general clean-up, renovating Ely House and Bann-a-boo House and their surrounding grounds. These two houses were later occupied by the officers. On 6 March, John O'Brien and six other servicemen arrived in Wexford at 11 p.m. John O'Brien writes in his diary:

> We were met at the train by Gunner Charles Rogers who accompanied us the three mile walk to what is to be an aviation station. We had coffee and sandwiches when we arrived and were shown to our beds for the night. We slept on the floor in Ely House, an old mansion.[4] Conditions are improving as we have moved into Bann-a-boo House and at last we have a soft bed to rest our weary bones.[5]

Working conditions were bad at Ferrybank: there was incessant rain and poor food, with breakfast consisting of one egg and two hard-tacks. John O'Brien and others worked from 8 a.m. to 5 p.m. in the pouring rain, with mud up to their knees, laying out the post holes for the barracks. 'Food is terrible, we don't get enough in the three meals-a-day to make up one good one,' John O'Brien commented. 'There was trouble in the camp to-day. The men all went on strike, and refused to work in the rain and mud without the proper clothes and half-starved.' On Saturday, 16 March, O'Brien wrote:

> Still raining, but I went ashore, After the movies, five of us stopped in at White's for a feed. I left at 10.45p.m. expecting to reach camp before liberty expired at 11p.m. I was ten minutes late. Beckett turned me in. Went before Rogers who claimed he could send me to Portsmith for 10 years. He couldn't send anyone to the brig for 10 minutes.

Discipline was rigid and the officers in charge really were hard on the men, considering the awful conditions they worked under to build the seaplane station. John O'Brien's diary entries are worth noting as they give a very informative insight into the life of a navy man serving in a strange country during wartime. John O'Brien possibly had some Irish roots, considering his name was O'Brien. On the next day, 17 March, St Patrick's Day, his diary records: 'I went to church and afterwards had a good dinner at White's Hotel. I spent the afternoon seeing Wexford and the country. Had an enjoyable day.'[6] Presumably, the Americans were not accustomed to such persistent downpours. O'Brien comments, 'Still raining. If this keeps up we will be all dead. It's still raining two days later. Riley went to hospital to-day. They think he has T.B.'[7]

The Americans took over Ely House[8] and Bann-a-boo[9] and quickly refurbished both houses, which were designated as officers' residences.

The inclement weather made the site a field of mud, but the men carried on the construction work against great odds, with insufficient sleep and various other handicaps. They got the work done. Competent judges claimed that the construction of the Wexford station set a record in the time it took to construct. It surpassed all other stations in England, France or Italy and it was the neatest, most up-to-date and otherwise the best station in Europe. This was a considerable tribute, considering that the men sent to the station had been enrolled just a few weeks before their arrival in Wexford, with the majority of them enrolled to carry out construction work only.

From the outset, the discipline was the same as on a ship and naval ideas and ideals and traditions were instilled into the men. Cleanliness, neatness and pride in the station were the watchwords. Upon the completion of the

Ely House – Officers' Quarters, Ferrybank, Wexford. (Canon S.S. de Vál)

Bann-a-boo House, Ferrybank, Wexford. (John Scanlon Photographic Archive)

station, it was obvious that warm comfortable barracks and an attractive mess hall where good food was plentiful fostered contentment and built up a morale that was known far and wide as the 'Wexford spirit'.[10]

Lieutenant Commander Victor Daniel Herbster arrived to take command of the base on the 5 April 1918.[11] The new commanding officer very quickly outlined to the men that he expected the work to be completed on the air base as quickly as possible, enabling the seaplanes to arrive at Ferrybank from Queenstown to commence detecting and destroying enemy submarines off the Wexford coast. He posted a round-the-clock work roster for the men to bring his plan into effect.[12] The strenuous workload saw the barracks completed and the storehouses erected towards the end of July. The air base had its own hospital and doctors, as well as a post office and meteorological station. At that time, Wexford town used gas for street lighting, but the Americans at Ferrybank had their own power-generating plant for electric lighting and other uses. Radio towers were essential for communication, especially when the seaplanes were in operation, even though the radio systems in the planes were not totally reliable.

WINGS OVER WEXFORD

Hangars at Ferrybank.

Washing drying on the hedgerow at the USN Station, Ferrybank. (USN Souvenir Book)

YMCA Hut, USN Air Station, Wexford. (Souvenir Book)

By August, there was still a considerable amount of work to be accomplished as the scheduled time for the arrival of the seaplanes was fast approaching. The contractors had finished the first hangar, the reservoir, the small water tank and the greater part of the internal roads and approach roads to the site. The water supply was connected and metered by Wexford Corporation at the going rate of water consumed. The base had a 60,000-gallon reserve water tank. The final departure of the civilian workforce occurred on 15 August. The speedy building of the second hangar and other buildings soon showed increased daily progress. The pier extension for the launch of the seaplanes was complete and practically all construction work on the base was finished.

The men took pride in their surroundings and built walkways and created grass plots, making the camp pleasing to the eye. The lifestyle at the air base had improved considerably, with athletics, baseball matches, football matches and boxing tournaments all encouraged.

The base had its own orchestra, which provided the music for some dances held on the base at their YMCA Hall. The Wexford *Free Press* reported on a boxing tournament in its 13 July issue, which makes for interesting reading. The tournament was held as part of the celebrations for Independence Day on 4 July:

Independence Day did not pass at Ferrybank without its boxing stunt, and the show provided at the Air Station in the evening was an enjoyable event. There was a large number of spectators present, due to the courtesy of the officers and men. The fair sex had the predominant position. The boxing took place in the Y.M.C.A. hut, and during the intervals the Station's Orchestra rendered some excellent music. The big crowd expected to see some classy contests, as it was rumoured that there were 'some mit slingers' amongst the 'White Caps', but in this they were disappointed, as the contests staged were of a very friendly and light nature. However, what was shown was interesting, and the trick sparring of Young Ritchie was enjoyed. There were three contests of three rounds each, and the first pair to face the music were Joe Fabula[13] and Carl Anderson. It was a good spar and the men received applause at the finish. The next pair in the 'circle' were Nugent of the USS Utah, and Allfrey[14] of New York. This was a lively bout. Nugent shot his left with effect into Alfrey's face and his nose showed 'red' as the result. Nugent appeared faster on his feet than Alfrey, though the latter showed a good knowledge of the game, but was slow. The home of the Tar Baby[15] and the late J. L. Sullivan,[16] Boston, produced Harry Mazzie,[17] and he sparred three rounds with a namesake of America's famous lightweight, Willie Ritchie,[18] Young Ritchie, a likely bit of goods though not possessing all the qualifications of the renowned Willie. These three rounds were excellent, and were greatly appreciated. Ritchie's trick of ducking and springing with a left to the face took the 'gods'. Mazzie shaped well, and with a little more experience should do well. The audience marked their appreciation of the men's handiness by loud applause. It was impossible to form an opinion as to the merits of the combatants as there was too much 'open glove' work, and 'here's my jaw' play. It would be interesting to witness Ferrybank's best in serious contests.

Baseball team, USNAS Wexford on sweaters. (USN Souvenir Book)

THE USN AIR BASE AT FERRYBANK

American Football team. (USN Souvenir Book)

Tennis party. USN officers with M.J. O'Connor and family. (O'Connor Collection)

The Ferrybank Air Station held baseball matches, as well as football matches, American style, against teams from other American stations in both home and away games. Such trips to County Cork were always special events for the teams. The competition between departments and between pilots was sharp and keen but always good-natured.[19] Many of the officers enjoyed visits to the home of well-known Wexford solicitor, Michael J. O'Connor, at Westlands, St John's Road for lawn tennis games.

Many lectures and talks were given from time to time, and one in particular was reported in the Wexford Notes of the *Free Press* newspaper on 24 August:

> A most interesting and attractive lecture, dealing with the Americans' attitude to the war. It was delivered in the American YMCA Hut at Ferrybank on Tuesday night under the presidency of Commander Herbster. The lecturer was Rev. Mr. Francis, a member of the American delegation which is presently touring the United Kingdom.

Labour Day, 2 September, was marked at the station, according to John J. O'Brien, 'with a regular old USA day with baseball, outdoor athletics finishing with a concert in the evening'.[20]

Ensign T. Harwood Stacey was the Intelligence Officer at Ferrybank and in O'Brien's diary entry for 18 September, he reports: 'To-day finds me a member of the Intelligence Section and kept busy getting acquainted with the code books and secret charts. I have had five cases to investigate including German spies in the Rosslare area. Went to a dance at Rosslare to investigate German spy.'[21] Security was very stringent during the war. All outgoing post from the air base was censored and very little, if any, information about the activities at the base was reported in the local newspapers; there was a total news blackout. Letters back home to America were permitted, but were subject to the strict censorship and mainly dealt with basic 'small talk' about family matters and loved ones. One such letter-writer was Chester McNichol. After the conclusion of the war and the signing of the Armistice, censorship restrictions were lifted and McNichol wrote a description of the USN Air Station in a letter to his friend:

> Here's a little about the camp. We've got five seaplanes and, of course, would have had more if the war had continued. Each is one hundred feet wide having two twelve cylinder motors. They look like a big fish and they certainly can cut the water, being able to land and rise from it. We have large places called hangars in which they are housed – each one holds four. When they are starting off, they first push them out like a boat, requiring about twenty men to do this. This you see after passing a sentry at the main gate. Just in the rear of this is a cave-like effect, where the depth charges are kept under guard. Two of these are carried on each plane, also five pigeons and four men. When I first came to this station there was only a couple of buildings in the place, so you see I'm an early settler, while now it's a small town. As we go back up the hill, first we

come to the machine shop, carpenter and blacksmith shops. Now we have the dynamo house where we get the juice for the camp. Then the post office and the brig where the naughty sailors are kept. Now we come to a whole street of barracks, the floors of these are painted slate colour, the beams white and the rest green, making it very nice inside. Also a stove, a table, chairs and lockers are therein. This is where we sleep. At the end of this street we find a storehouse in which all the eats are stored. Opposite this is the kitchen or galley where the food is cooked. Adjoining this is the messhall where four hundred sailors are fed three times daily. Now we come to the sick bay, three doctors and four assistants, a building with a lot of bedding, etc. Now we go into the Y.M.C.A., across the street is the canteen and another street of barracks.

Back of these is the wireless station consisting of two poles about as high as the town-pump, a lot of wires and a small building. Further along we have the lookout facing the bay and the pigeon house of which there is about a hundred in the flock. Down the hill to the left is the garage, three six-ton Packard's, five Rainier trucks and trailers, three Fords, two Cadillac touring cars and two motorcycles. Walking back a little we come to the different department offices all in one string of buildings. That covers it roughly. This station has been passed as the best air station in Europe.[22]

In the souvenir booklet outlining the history of the Wexford air station, the author writes that the station was organised and had been built and equipped for just one purpose: to fight and destroy the German submarines in the seas around the Wexford coast.[23] The American forces proved to be very successful in this battle.

By August of 1918, there was still work to be completed, as it was almost time for the arrival of the seaplanes from their base at Queenstown. The civilian workmen were dismissed on 15 August. The work on the erection of the second hangar started immediately and rapid progress was made, until construction was forced to stop due to the shortage of buildings materials. Work was being carried out on every part of the station, with noticeable progress being made on an almost daily basis. The men worked day and night shifts on the large 60,000-gallon reserve water tank, which was almost as large as a tennis court. The same Trojan work was being carried out on the pier extension adjacent to the slipway. The pile-driver could be heard hammering twenty-four hours a day across the waters of the river.[24]

Over the weeks, small drafts of men had been transferred from Aghada, Co. Cork, and by 1 July the numbers at the site had reached 232 men and

13 officers, increasing to 298 men and 15 officers by 1 August. Finally, there were 410 men and 20 officers at the base, plus 8 other personnel, including: a radio officer; boatswain; assistant engineer officer; public works officer; electrical officer; ordnance officer; YMCA secretary and YMCA assistant secretary. There was a total of 438 personnel at the station by the end of October.[25] Everything was ready to engage in battle with the German U-boats.

Sentries at Ely House gate. (USN Souvenir Book)

Liberty boat at Ferrybank, Wexford, 1918. (Michael Kavanagh)

5

Wings over Wexford

On Wednesday, 18 September, four Curtiss H-16 seaplanes left from Aghada, County Cork, on their way to Ferrybank, Wexford. Just three of the seaplanes arrived safely; the fourth aircraft crashed and was damaged beyond repair during the flight. This marked the transition of the men from construction workers to a fully operational team of naval personnel. The commitment and enthusiasm of the men resulted in a smooth and effective changeover. The following day, the seaplanes took flight for their first patrol, which continued every day afterwards, as long as the weather conditions permitted flying.

In late 1917, the Allied forces introduced the convoy system, which reduced losses of shipping due to attacks by U-boats. The German commanders changed their tactics, concentrating on shipping headed for the main ports of Great Britain, with major losses off the south-west coast. To combat these attacks by the U-boats, the US anti-submarine air patrols covered the sea areas from Wexford, including the entrance to the Bristol Channel and the Irish Sea in a northerly direction as far as Liverpool. These patrols also covered the seas off the south coast of Ireland as far as Cork Harbour, all within a radius of 100 miles of Wexford.

At least two seaplanes were available on a daily basis for patrol duty in spite of shortages of spare parts or accidental damage to the planes. One such accident occurred when one of the pilots taxied his plane up Wexford Harbour in a high tide and, in an effort to take a short-cut by clearing one of the breakwaters, embedded his aircraft in the rocky ridge, causing damage to the hull.

On 21 September, a mere three days after the anti-submarine patrols had begun, a German U-boat was sighted and attacked by H-16 A1079 from

Pilots sitting on the bow of seaplane at USN Station, Ferrybank. (Delaney Collection)

Testing motors before a flight. (USN Souvenir Book)

Curtiss H-16 with Wexford town in background. (Delaney Collection)

Wexford. Two bombs were dropped close to the submarine, both of which exploded and damaged the submarine.

Contact was maintained with the station by a wireless installation monitored from the high towers at Ferrybank. For safety in the event of wireless failure, the planes also had carrier pigeons, which would have been used to carry vital information back to the air base. A few years prior to the outbreak of war, early aviators relied on homing pigeons as a reliable means of communication between aircraft and stations set close to the shoreline. It was felt by the US Navy Department that the pigeons might be able to save the lives of airmen stranded on the sea, a long distance from the shore and safety.[1] The pigeon lofts at Ferrybank housed over 100 homing birds, which were released as a test from time to time and in several instances proved their worth in emergencies. Before pigeons could be used to any great advantage, special training methods had to be adopted as the careful training of the birds was invaluable to the entire operation.

Taught to fly home over increasingly long distances over water, many pigeons were lost while attempting these long flights, much to the frustration of their handlers. The message carriers had to contend with extreme weather conditions and battled against strong winds, heavy fog, torrential rain and sleet, yet most of the birds made their way home to base.[2] Finding enough on-board storage space for the pigeons created another problem, which was eventually solved by placing the birds in boxes in the front cockpit of the larger bombers and in a special container installed on the floats of the smaller planes.[3]

Ferrybank, located on Wexford Harbour, was an ideal location for the air base. It was sheltered and well protected from wind and weather within the almost land-locked harbour and the waters were basically calm. The wide expanse of water, free from obstruction, allowed for the safe take-off and landing of the huge seaplanes. The only bridge crossing the river, giving

Wexford Bridge at Carcur. (Lawrence Collection, National Library of Ireland)

access to the town, was further up the river at Carcur. The seaplanes would have easily risen skywards before reaching the Ballast Bank situated in the river just opposite the southern end of the quay front.[4]

A seaplane patrolling more than 30 miles seawards carried at least two pigeons on board. Messages to be sent from the aircraft were written on onion skin paper[5] and inserted into a small aluminium capsule fastened to one of the pigeon's legs before it was set loose in the hope that it would find its way back to the pigeon loft. Much to the US Naval Department's relief, many brave pigeons did find their way back to base, carrying vital messages, which brought help and salvation to stricken pilots. The unfamiliar sight of airborne seaplanes and a flock of pigeons over Wexford must have provoked surprise among the inhabitants of the town and surrounding countryside. Submarine activity had increased off south Wexford resulting in more and more air patrols flying from Ferrybank, as noted by John O'Brien in his diary as follows: 'On Thursday 3 October, two sea-planes went on patrol today and on Saturday due to rain the planes were grounded as reports came into the communications centre of four submarines were sighted in the area.'[6]

Later in October, another seaplane arrived at Ferrybank to replace one of the original four planes that had been damaged before delivery. Soon after the commencement of operations and regular patrol flights, the first submarine was bombed, putting it out of action. On Friday, 11 October, following the sinking of the *Leinster*, one of the Wexford planes spotted and bombed

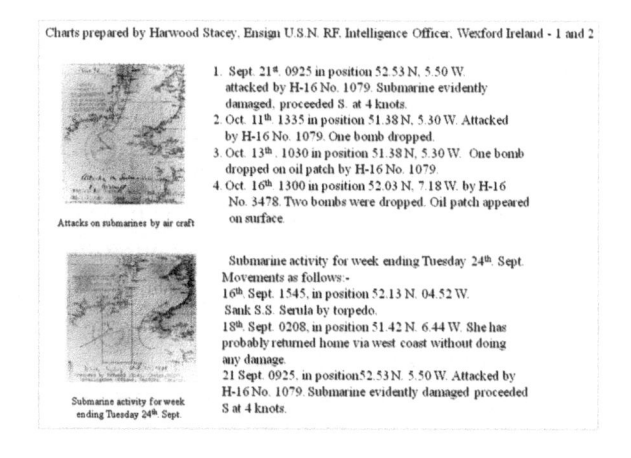

Charts prepared by Harwood Stacey, Nos 1 and 2. (Naval History and Heritage Command (NHHC))

Charts prepared by Harwood Stacey, Ensign U.S.N. RF. Intelligence Officer, Wexford Ireland - 1 and 2

Attacks on submarines by air craft

1. Sept. 21st. 0925 in position 52.53 N, 5.50 W. attacked by H-16 No. 1079. Submarine evidently damaged, proceeded S. at 4 knots.
2. Oct. 11th 1335 in position 51.38 N, 5.30 W. Attacked by H-16 No. 1079. One bomb dropped.
3. Oct. 13th. 1030 in position 51.38 N, 5.30 W. One bomb dropped on oil patch by H-16 No. 1079.
4. Oct. 16th. 1300 in position 52.03 N, 7.18 W. by H-16 No. 3478. Two bombs were dropped. Oil patch appeared on surface.

Submarine activity for week ending Tuesday 24th. Sept.

Submarine activity for week ending Tuesday 24th. Sept. Movements as follows:-
16th. Sept. 1545, in position 52.13 N. 04.52 W. Sank S.S. Serula by torpedo.
18th. Sept. 0208, in position 51.42 N. 6.44 W. She has probably returned home via west coast without doing any damage.
21 Sept. 0925. in position 52.53 N. 5.50 W. Attacked by H-16 No. 1079. Submarine evidently damaged proceeded S at 4 knots.

Charts prepared by Harwood Stacey, Nos 3 and 4. (Naval History and Heritage Command (NHHC))

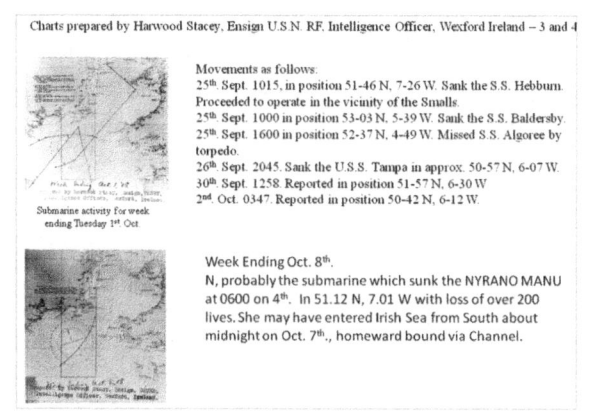

Charts prepared by Harwood Stacey, Ensign U.S.N. RF. Intelligence Officer, Wexford Ireland – 3 and 4

Submarine activity for week ending Tuesday 1st. Oct.

Movements as follows:
25th. Sept. 1015, in position 51-46 N, 7-26 W. Sank the S.S. Hebburn. Proceeded to operate in the vicinity of the Smalls.
25th. Sept. 1000 in position 53-03 N, 5-39 W. Sank the S.S. Baldersby.
25th. Sept. 1600 in position 52-37 N, 4-49 W. Missed S.S. Algoree by torpedo.
26th. Sept. 2045. Sank the U.S.S. Tampa in approx. 50-57 N, 6-07 W.
30th. Sept. 1258. Reported in position 51-57 N, 6-30 W
2nd. Oct. 0347. Reported in position 50-42 N, 6-12 W.

Week Ending Oct. 8th.
N, probably the submarine which sunk the NYRANO MANU at 0600 on 4th. In 51.12 N, 7.01 W with loss of over 200 lives. She may have entered Irish Sea from South about midnight on Oct. 7th., homeward bound via Channel.

an enemy submarine off the Wexford coast. Following the bombing, the U-boat had difficulty submerging. Later, thick black oil coated the surface of the water and lasted for about a week after the attack. It was proof that the perpetrators of the *Leinster* sinking had been punished for their crime.

Five days after this bombing, on Wednesday, 16 October, a seaplane, piloted by Lieutenant John F. McNamara with Ensign J.R. Biggs as second pilot and Ensign George W. Shaw as observer, on patrol from the Queenstown air base, spotted a periscope projecting above the waves on its way to Wexford. Hovering for thirty minutes, the H-16 seaplane dropped a bomb, which failed to explode, but a second drop exploded very close to the periscope, which disappeared from sight. Over the coming days, bombs were dropped and by the end of the month submarines were noticeably scarce in the area.[7]

By Wednesday, 6 November, a fifth seaplane was at the station. Had the war continued, the number of seaplanes scheduled to serve at Ferrybank was to be brought to eighteen. With just five planes in service at the Wexford station, their orders were to patrol for as many hours as possible during daylight, with all repair and overhaul work carried out during the night to ensure the fleet was ready at all times to deal with all eventualities. This meant that the service crews often worked eighteen hours continually, for days at a time, ensuring the planes received expert care and maintenance. In spite of the absence of spare parts, the service crews managed to have two seaplanes ready for anti-submarine patrols every day during daylight hours. It is on record that flying personnel serving at Ferrybank were not involved in a single accident. Safety was paramount.

From the beginning of operations at the base at Wexford on 18 September until 11 November, the five seaplanes made a total of 98 flights spread over 312 flying hours, clocking up 19,135 sea miles patrolled. During the month of October, Ferrybank-based seaplanes destroyed four submarines, a

Tuskar Rock Lighthouse, Wexford. (Brian O'Hagan)

commendable record of success. Pilots were able to fly on days that would otherwise have been written off thanks to the Intelligence Department and the mapping of complete courses with compass corrections and wind deflections, and reliable information from the Meteorological Department. The Wexford location played a major role from a strategic point of view as the Ferrybank station lay directly at the southern entrance to the Irish Sea, just 12 miles from Tuskar Rock Lighthouse.

Tuskar Rock Lighthouse is one of the most important navigational markers in British waters. During the four years of the First World War, many ships were attacked and sunk by enemy submarines within a short distance from the Rock and in full view of the lighthouse keepers. Due to the large number of shipping losses, this particular area of sea was sadly known as 'The Graveyard of Ships'. All Allied shipping had to pass through these waters en route to and from England and the German U-boats used the Irish Sea as a short route to and from their bases, making it the perfect place for extensive submarine activities.

The seaplane patrols made attacks on shipping a difficult task for enemy submarines and so there were fewer marine losses. The seaplanes flown in Ireland were the H-16 design, and by 1917 this series of aircraft was at the pinnacle of its design: its longer wing span and stronger hull allowed for much better control of the aircraft's overall larger dimensions. At the commencement of the First World War, the airplane was still in its formative development and design stages, and it was regarded as a novelty as it had a very limited flying range and required constant repair and engine servicing. In contrast to this, the German zeppelin was more reliable and effective as a flying machine capable of wreaking havoc on shipping, military installations and English and French cities.

On its entry into the war, the US Navy's air strength was comprised of 48 officers, 239 enlisted men, 54 training planes, a couple of balloons, one dirigible and just one air station and training centre at Pensacola, Florida. It was 1916 before the American government provided approximately $4 million for the US Navy's first flying corps.[8]

The H-16 seaplane was built mainly of timber. The frames of the planes were constructed from spruce wood. In a series of articles published in the *New York Herald*, one of its contributors, Frank Parker Stockbridge, described the construction of the US Navy's newest weapon:

The entire fabric of an airplane is composed of struts, stretchers, stresses and strains. The incredibly light and thin veneers, glued together were strong like steel. As delicate as a grasshopper's wings, the transverse webs that shape the wings of an airplane are carved from the thinnest of boards, and yet, under the strain of piano-wire braces, they hold like rigid iron. The secret was straight-grained, seasoned spruce and glue.

Ordinary glue, made of hoofs, horns and hides from slaughterhouses was not strong enough to hold airplanes together. In hot conditions the animal glue melted and the planes literally fell apart. Casein, a by-product of skim milk, turned into a glue solved the problem. Another problem was a suitable material to cover the wings of the plane with, the only kind of cloth suitable being Irish linen made from flax. The fabric was extremely durable and did not rip apart when punctured. Ireland could not supply flax in the quantities required by both America and England so once again American scientists set out to find a substitute for flax. Sea-island cotton was the answer. To meet the demand the American Government commandeered the large cotton mills at Falls River, Massachusetts to manufacture the new cloth. The mills turned out nearly eight million yards of the fabric. It wore like iron and was almost waterproof and was a perfect substitute for Irish linen.

Flying a seaplane was completely different from piloting a land-based aircraft. In order to withstand the additional stress of taking off and landing on water the plane had to be of a very sturdy construction. The difficulties for aviators learning to fly a seaplane included calm seas and little wind, as the aircraft needed to travel faster than ground-speed before enough load was taken off the wing floats and it became airborne. As a result, flying a seaplane, especially during wartime, became a nightmare for many of the very young and almost inexperienced aviators.[9]

It is probable that onlookers standing on Wexford quayside in 1918 would have witnessed seaplanes struggling across the surface of the water like great albatrosses with clipped wings trying to attain sufficient speed to lift off. On one occasion, a pilot who was taxiing his seaplane up the harbour during a high tide attempted to make a short-cut across one of the breakwaters which was barely covered by water. He lodged the hull of his plane in the rocky ridge of the breakwater, necessitating major repair.

Many aviators managed to take off without any problem, while others would taxi continuously until all the water in the radiators of their engines had boiled away. Overseeing all of these successes and mishaps was Lieutenant

Commander Victor Daniel Herbster. During his tenure in Wexford, he had sole responsibility for the air base and all its activities.

The original paint colour of the H-16 was opaque yellow, but during the war years the naval aircraft wings were painted with an English khaki grey enamel, which gave good camouflage to the plane. The US government aircraft were obliged to carry a distinguishing insignia on the wings, consisting of a red disc within a white star on a blue circular field. Red, white and blue vertical stripes were painted on the plane's rudder, with the colour blue in the first position of the colour scheme. Each aircraft was identifiable by three inch-high figures showing the building number of each plane. These numbers were displayed at the top of a white vertical band on the rudder. As the cockpits of the seaplanes were relatively open to the elements, the pilots wore a tan sheepskin long coat over a short coat and trousers with moleskin hood and goggles. The entire flight clothing also had black leather gloves, soft leather boots, waders, brogans[10] and a lifebelt for each member of the seaplane's crew.

In total, the USN Air Station was in operation for just eight weeks before it closed down following the signing of the Armistice on 11 November 1918. Most of the trainee pilots stationed at Ferrybank qualified as first-class pilots after the intensive instruction they received while on regular patrols in their

Launching a H-16 seaplane.

H-16s. In total, 478 of the H series were eventually produced. They were retired soon after the war ended and replaced with more modern types of aircraft.

During those few weeks in 1918, Wexford town heard the mighty roar of the seaplane engines as they took flight from the river waters, heading out on their quest to find the enemy submarines that were causing such mayhem in the seas around the coast. The expertise and diligence of the American pilots and crews very soon halted the progress of the iron fish that had invaded the Irish Sea and St George's Channel.

As the photograph demonstrates, launching a H-16 required the strength of at least twenty men, who held the heavy ropes and gradually allowed the plane to roll down towards the water. The seaplane sat on a small wooden bogey equipped with wheels, giving momentum to the launching as the plane lurched along the slipway in readiness for take-off. Some of the service crew entered the water to ensure that the guide ropes were released from the aircraft and the bogey was pulled back onto the slipway – a dangerous task for all involved, including the pilot and his crew.

On a return flight to Ferrybank, the H-16 would have landed a distance away from the slipway and taxied to meet the waiting launch and retrieval crew. The work of pulling the seaplane back up the incline of the slipway was backbreaking and required the full strength of the twenty men. The seaplane had to be pulled across the roadway and safely berthed in one of the four large aircraft hangars to await the repair and service crews to ensure it was ready to take flight again in another submarine hunt.

Had the war continued beyond 1918 and the expected complement of seaplanes, eighteen in number, arrived for duty in Wexford, the numbers of officers and men would have far exceeded the 438 already at the air station.

Following the signing of the Armistice, the US Naval Air Stations were no longer required. All anti-submarine patrols by seaplanes were discontinued and the planes were grounded and disarmed. Construction work still in progress ended immediately and the demobilisation of personnel and the dismantling of the buildings commenced. Just twelve days after the Armistice was signed, 200 men were on their way home from Wexford and the evacuation of the men continued until well into December. A small contingent of men remained to prepare and pack tools, instruments, medical equipment, motor transport, mess gear, seaplane engine spare parts and other

Pulling a Curtiss H-16 ashore. (Delaney Collection)

important and valuable equipment. All items were shipped out via Dublin for America.

British naval officers visited the US Naval Air Stations in Ireland and surveyed them for possible future use by the Royal Navy. Wexford was not required for future British defence plans. Following this rejection of the site at Ferrybank by the Royal Navy, it was determined that all buildings and other installations had to be removed either by shipment back to America or sold locally before the US Navy could leave the area. The four large aircraft hangars were sold to business firms in the town of Wexford, with some of them surviving until the mid-1970s before they were finally demolished. The US Naval Air Station at Ferrybank finally closed in February 1919, bringing to a close the American occupation of a part of Wexford.

It was early in 1919 that Commander Victor D. Herbster left the USN Air Base at Ferrybank, his work completed. He had gained considerable experience with the fledgling air corps of the US Navy, having registered for flight instruction at the Aviation Camp at Annapolis in November 1911. It was at this camp that Ensign Herbster trained in flying and qualified as

Naval Aviator No. 5 on 1 July 1914. Ensign Herbster was soon working with Glenn Hammond Curtis, carrying out experimental flights in the Curtiss flying boats and other airplanes. Commander Herbster quickly rose through the ranks, achieving the rank of Lieutenant Commander, and in 1918 he was assigned to command the air station at Wexford. He was awarded one of the navy's highest honours from the President of the United States of America. The citation read as follows:

> The Navy Cross is awarded to Lieutenant Commander Victor D. Herbster, U.S. Navy, for distinguished service in the line of his profession in command of the Armed Guard of the U.S.S. St. Louis, where his good judgement and quick action probably saved that ship from being torpedoed on three occasions, and in one case resulted in sinking of an enemy submarine. Later as commanding

Lieut. Commander Victor Daniel Herbster. (Noland Collection)

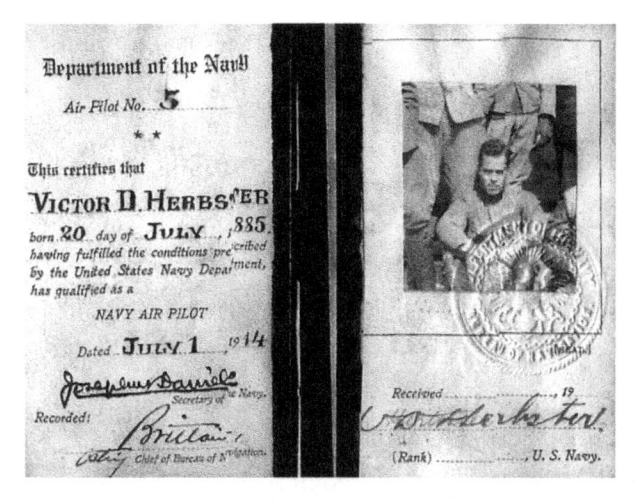

Victor D. Herbster, Navy Air Pilot No. 5, 1 July 1914. (Noland Collection)

officer of the U.S. Naval Air Station, Wexford, Ireland, he rendered valuable service in establishing and operating same.

Victor Daniel Herbster eventually served forty years with the US Navy and retired, with the rank of captain, in 1945, to his home in Norwich, Connecticut. Victor Herbster was born 20 July 1885. He died just one year after his retirement, on Friday, 6 December 1946, aged 61, at the Naval Hospital, St Alban's, New York. He was survived by his wife, the former Cathleen Nolan, a native of Dublin, and his two daughters. He was the son of the Reverend Samuel and Mrs Herbster.

6

The Officers and Crew

Lieut. Comdr Victor D. Herbster, USN, Commanding
Lieut. (jg) Clarence B. Tillotson, USNRF, Executive Officer
Lieut. (jg) John F. McNamara, USNRF, Senior Flight Officer
Lieut. (jg) William S. Vanderbilt, USNRF, Meteorological Officer
Lieut. (jg) George W. Shaw, USNRF, Pilot
Ensign T. Harwood Stacy, USNRF, Intelligence Officer
Ensign Charles L. Vaughan, USNRF, Engineer Officer
Ensign Ralph A. Lehan, USNRF, Pilot
Ensign Howard A. Beswick, USNRF, Pilot
Ensign Edward T. Garvey, USNRF, Pilot
Ensign H, McLean Purdy, USNRF, Pilot
Ensign Paul E. Froass, USNRF, Pilot
Ensign Charles V. Brady, USNRF, Pilot
Ensign Harry H. Hunter, USNRF, Pilot
Ensign Paul Raymer, USNRF, Pilot
Ensign Robert B. Wilcox, USNRF, Pilot
Boatswain Rush H. Reed, USN, Boatswain

Officers and Crew

Officers and Crew, USN Air Station, Wexford.

THE OFFICERS AND CREW

Gunner Charles A. Rogers, USN, Radio Officer
Machinist Carl F. Nolting, USN, Asst. Engineer Officer
Lieut. (MC) Phillip S. Sullivan, USN, Senior Medical Officer
Lieut. (MC) William B. James, USN, Asst Medical Officer
Ensign (PC) Ralph E. Morton, USNRF, Pay and Supply Officer
Ensign (PC) William T. Ross, USN, Asst Supply Officer
Carpenter Thomas A. Clark, USN, Public Works Officer
Chief Electrician William H. Lloyd, USNRF, Electrical Officer
Chief Gunner's Mate William L. Beckett, USNRF, Ordnance Officer
Doctor Evor Evans, YMCA Secretary
Mr J.E. Talbot, YMCA Asst Secretary

Chief Boatswain's Mate:
Timothy M. Donovan

Chief Gunner's Mates:
William L. Beckett
Myer E. Collins
Olin F. Johnson

Chief Quartermasters:
Charles F. Bertschinger
Ruy H. Finch
John Lushear
Roswell L. Tice

Chief Machinist Mates:
Herman Albertine
Frank J. Brower
James A. Busch
Thomas F. Crowley
Roy P. Gates
Anderson T. Fivey
Harold E. Menard

Chief Electricians (Radio):
Glenn W. Curtiss
Lindley A. Killie

Chief Electricians (General):
William H. Lloyd
Ray Strohl

Chief Carpenter's Mates:
Thomas R. Allfrey
John P. Dolbec
Thomas R. Doody
Archie C. Goddard
Joseph R. Gordon
Adolph W. Lottman
James M. Murphy
John J. O'Brien
Joseph F. Pistone
Charles E. Riley

Chief Yeomen:
Earl T. Mitchell
Gates Murchie

Chief Storekeepers:
William English
Charles E. Spencer

Chief Pharmacist's Mate:
Carl J. Stommel

Commissary Stewart:
Albert J. Jarvis

Boatswain's Mate 1st Class:
William G. Crowley

Gunner's Mate 1st Class:
William J. Daly.

Quartermasters 1st Class:
Edwin W. Blue
Marcus L. Critchlow
Joseph F. Curry
Thomas A. Fitzpatrick
Colin McLennan
Jesse E. McClellan
John F. Price
Harold H. Sandel
Reynold A. Strom
John E. Tolman
Arthur G. Volbrecht
Rufe L. Wallace
Thomas C. Warren
Charles S. Webber
James A. Wise
John A. Zafian

Machinist Mates 1st Class:
John Beck
Jasper Bennett
Frank C. Dedon
Roy H. Grant
Harold L. Gilliatt
Alfred W. Hanson
Harry Kennedy
Jack Levin
Basil P. McCarthy
William A. MacDonald

Williard H. Marshall
Lucian J. Martin
Joseph R. Mullin
Walter Niehans
Francis P. O'Brien
Harold O. Phillips
Harold C. Safford
Chris G. Schroeder
John L. Sweeney
John M. Zell

Electricians 1st Class (Radio):
Wallace M. Frazier
Edwin C. Gustafson
John R. Haraldson
Lloyd M. Patterson
Glow B. Phillips
Gordon L. Wallace

Electricians 1st Class (General):
Henry Asher
Charles W. Burney
John H. Driscoll
James F. Fagan
Charles H. Greenfield
Leonard Lyons
George T. Morgan
Matthias A. Nugent
Robert Rohrbough
Howard Steffens
Jerome Stembel

Carpenter's Mates 1st Class:
James W. Bartlett
Martin Berg
Michael A. Bosch
William Burke
John A. Campbell

THE OFFICERS AND CREW

Martin J. Collins
Edwin Crossfield
James T. Curr
Panfilo Delle Donne
Edward J. Duncan;
William J. Geach
Daniel Geelan
George D. Green
Louis F. Healey
Merrill J. Henley
James P. Hinman
Charles Jacobs
Gordon E. James
Thomas J. Kelley
Edward W. Kenny
Calvin P. Linsley
Henry C. McCarthy
Joseph McCloskey
Eric W. Malmstrom
Frank A. Merkel
Thomas J. Mullen
Albert C. Morrison
Chris W. Schlesser
Joel E. Smith

Ship Fitters 1st Class:
Francis J. Boasa
William P. Coughlin
Joseph P. Dooner
Clarence C. Ellsworth
Henry W. Ellsworth
Raymond Halleran
Thomas F. Kerwin
Henry Miller
Patrick J. Qualey
John Ryan
John M. Vedder
Anthony L. Walke

Boilermakers:
Jeremiah L. Curtin
Thomas A. Walsh

Plummer and Fitter:
Edward P. Morris

Coppersmiths 1st Class:
James J. Daly
Charles Davidson
Roland R. Reeder

Blacksmiths 1st Class:
William M. Claydon
John J. Jud
John Mathias

Yeomen 1st Class:
Arthur E. Becker
Cornelius J. Driscoll
Roger J. Gallagher
Edward A. Mackin
Abraham M. Parnes
John G. Styler

Storekeeper 1st Class:
Leo B. Welch

Ship's Cooks 1st Class:
Robert Y. Clark
Herman A. Lindemann
Chester J. McNichol
Edgar D. Morris

Bakers 1st Class:
John Fischer
Charles E. Melcher

Pharmacist Mate 1st Class:
William F. Moore

Painter 1st Class:
Osmond R. Tweet

Printer 1st Class:
Hugh W. Smith

Boatswain's Mate 2nd Class:
Carl C. Perolio

Gunner's Mate 2nd Class:
Frank W. Dubia

Quartermasters 2nd Class:
Ray Asher
Bernard T. Cleary
William F. Coleman
Thomas J. Curry
William A. Dennard
Rolland A. Estes
Frank W. Flarity
Orville J. Gload
William H. Glover
Richard Grainger
Lester E. McCormack
Edward R. McIvor
John A. McLaughlin
Stanley A. Mansfield
Harry Moran
William C. Moss
Chauncey R.E. Norris
Arthur F. O'Connell
Oliver C. Schneider
Harold C. Sheehy
Stanley A. Stokes
Patrick T. Sullivan

Gabriel L. Sultan
Herbert E. Swan
Harry H. Weaver
Roman D. Webb
Charlie H. Woodis

Machinist Mates 2nd Class:
Frederick Battell
Walter E. Bernitz
James L. Blake
James A. Boal
Eli A. Boosahda
Victor R. Bradford
Frank P. Brazell
Edward L. Comontopski
Paul G. Cronin
James F. Daly
Harry C. Gray
Herman P. Hopkins
William S. Jordan
Edward G. Kelley
Charles A. McKenna
William McMeekin
Merton F. McNair
John P. Malloy
Harry A. Mazzie
John B. Miller
Charles A. Osteritter
Martin Podraza
Otto D. Raffaelle
William H. Schreckenstein
Ernest G. Soderstrom
Willis G. Yarbrough

Electricians 2nd Class (Radio):
Alvin T. Bates
Karl F. Clark
Joel R. Cornett

George DeW. Goodrich
Richard S. Goodrich
Harvey A. Hesser
Harry H. Houston
James M. Larkins
Leslie W. McClure
Charles D. Rosenfeld
George C. Ross
Marcus K. Selig
Wilfred L. Shaw
Howard McK. Young

Electricians 2nd Class (General):
Robert Bartlett
Thomas J. Norris
John Sale

Carpenter's Mates 2nd Class:
William Aitken Jr
Earl C. Brower
Thomas J. Cleary
Michael Darcy
William Eaton
Richard L. Fairbrother
Frank A. Flood
Charles S. Flynn
Mark Hannon
Ross C. Haughey
Herman R. Hellwig
Frederick W. Konerding
Ollie A. Ley
Angus Lyons
Linfred S. Newhart

Coppersmiths 2nd Class:
John P. Callaghan

Ship Fitters 2nd Class:
Anthony J. Ferrulle
Aaron Franzblau
Charles A. Hume
Louis D. Russell

Blacksmiths 2nd Class:
William B. Galbraith
James L. Grove
Edward Hanson
Roland Hilderbrant
Anthony W. Lineman Jr
Parker H. Lyman
John H. McAlinden
Arthur A. Pritchard

Yeomen 2nd Class:
William F. Butters
Henry R. Mead
Lloyd A. Murphy
Edwin G. Patterson

Storekeepers 2nd Class:
Joseph Fickinger
George R. Gill
Joseph Hampl Jr
Michael F. Mullane
Murray B. Parks
Richard J. Snell

Ship's Cooks 2nd Class:
James M. Collings
Amos B. Johnson
Joseph A. Knudsen
Henry Rice

Bakers 2nd Class:
Harry Barthel

Lester E. Cone
John J. Havelick
Edward Westman

Pharmacist Mate 2nd Class:
Wilfred C. Stroud

Coxswains:
James F. Bennett
Robert S. Wilkinson

Quartermasters 3rd Class:
Charles P. Graham
William M. Hooks

Electricians 3rd Class (Radio):
Joseph H. Kirchmann
Burham D. Lapham
Charles J. McNab
Oliver C. Miller
Benjamin C. Nourse
Albert L. Percival
Charles A. Scrivner
Leroy C. Townsend
Isaac B. Williams

Carpenter's Mates 3rd Class:
Bennie Batson
Henry Batson
Abe Boersema
Ernest M. Bozak
John Burke
Clarence E. Burns
Thure A. Cerling
Joseph Corkery
Albert S. Dilks
Whitney G. Dumesnil
Sherman Eichles

Harry E. Ferris
Charles Fritz
Ewald J. Hinz
John J. Hogan
John B. Jenkins
Samuel Kassel
Charles L. Kaudy
Emile A. Landry
Richard S. Maybin
Edward Meinhold
Henry A. Muller

Painters 3rd Class:
Arthur F. Slavin
Frank G. Sliwa

Pharmacist Mates 3rd Class:
Wayne Luce
Joseph W. Stevens

Ship's Cooks 3rd Class:
Frank Clegg
William E. Murray

Hospital Apprentice 1st Class:
David D. Inglis

Seamen:
Leonard G. Allbaugh
McKinley Armstrong
Eugene T. Coutellier
Charles E. Crenshaw
Nathan C. Eason
Joseph M. Fabula
Ernst A. Galland
Harry I. Hoover
John Huber
Floyd H. Johnson

THE OFFICERS AND CREW

Theron R. Jones
George F. Killian
Raymond L. King
Albert L. Kletsch
Frank Kotalik Jr
Lawson McCardel
Raymund Manier
Victor B. Robb
Albert C. Sax
Robert R. Schuelke
Willard L. Scott
Thomas M. Skophammer
Otto Steinbach Jr

Firemen 1st Class:
Stelios Belazero
Edgar R. Carlson
Harry G. Frericks
John Hourihan
James J. Peters
John J. Warford

Ship's Cook 4th Class:
Hugo C. Koeth

Seamen 2nd Class:
George E. Agal
Eugene B. Alberter
William Bridgeman
Richard A. Clark
Herman W. Cole
Milo Conner
Oscar T. Crader
Joseph J. Darino
William J. Dibbert
Oscar D. Draxten
Joseph W. Firstel
Herbert F.A. Flatter

George Frezon
Earl Gard
Harvey H. Garman
George W. Gilde
William H. Greenwell
Raymond E. Harden
Raymond E. Hebenstreit
Edsell C. Jones
Bernard A. Kean
Frank L. Kleban
Thomas C. Kleczka
John Klimazewski
Michael L. Krueger
Lawrence E. Lafave
Leonard Lundry
John H. McCray
Daniel J. Mallette
James F. Marek
Ryland T. Miller
John D. Naughton
Mike Nerad
Patrick J. Nerney
Louis F. Olberding
Edward D. Owen
William W. Parker
Thomas C. Perkins
Alfred A. Peterson
Charles J. Quinn
Johnie A. Reiter
George H. Retter
Edward Reynolds
Robert B. Roddy
Louis M. Samuels
Fred Schnell
John Schweitzer
Custer E. Seckinger
Edward Seefurth
Fred J. Seidewand

George D. Tyrone
Archie H. Young

Firemen 2nd Class:
Franklin P. Connell
Vallie L. Erwin
Harry A. Lowe
Carl Mayfield

Firement 3rd Class:
Phillip G. Hayes

Wardroom Steward:
George W. Tyson

Mess Attendants 1st Class:
Wilton Haywood
Thornton Riser
John Tayloe
Roosevelt Wimes

The crew roll totalled 410 men, of 61 different ranks, including boatswains, gunners, quartermasters, machinists, electricians, radio electricians, carpenters, yeomen, storekeepers, pharmacist, commissary steward, ship fitters, boilermakers, plumber and fitter, coppersmiths, blacksmiths, ship's cooks, bakers, painter, printer, hospital staff, seamen, firemen, wardroom steward and mess attendants. The various ranks were classed from first to fourth class.

The USN Air Base at Ferrybank, Wexford, also had the additional staff of twenty men, including the commanding officer, officers, pilots and eight other servicemen, making a total of 438 men serving at the air base at Ferrybank by the end of October 1918. The entire personnel at Ferrybank were under the command of Lieutenant Commander Victor Daniel Herbster.

THE OFFICERS AND CREW

OFFICERS

Lieut.(jg.) John F. McNamara
Lieut.(jg.) George W. Shaw
Ensign Paul E. Froass
Lieut. Comdr. Victor D. Herbster
Ensign Howard A. Beswick
Ensign Paul H. Raymer
Ensign Edward T. Garvey
Ensign A.H. McCormick
Ensign Charles L. Vaughan

Cmdr V.D. Herbster and officers at USN Air Station, Ferrybank, Wexford, 1918.

Officers at USN Air Station Ferrybank, Wexford. (Delaney Collection)

WINGS OVER WEXFORD

Pioneers; Transportation; Radio Electricians; General Electricians. (Delaney Collection)

Public Works; Boatswains; Q-Masters; Engineers Dept. (Delaney Collection)

THE OFFICERS AND CREW

Seaman Guard; Commissary Dept, Crew Mess Men; Mess-Boys. (Delaney Collection)

Sick-Bay; Ward of Sick-Bay; Mail-O; Medical Staff. (Delaney Collection)

7

Rosslare Listens

Rosslare Harbour is located at the end of the N25, twenty minutes from Wexford town.[1] Due to its location and its relative proximity to Fishguard in Wales (62.77 miles away), it was an ideal place to set up a wireless telegraphy station.[2] Even prior to the First World War, the nearby village of Rosslare Strand served as the very first wireless telegraphy station in south-east Wexford. Early in 1901, Guglielmo Marconi began his experimentation, attempting to transmit a signal across the Atlantic. If he was successful, he could compete with the transatlantic telegraph cables. As part of this effort, Marconi set up a transmitting station in Marconi House at Rosslare Strand, Co. Wexford. It was to act as a link between Poldhu in Cornwall, England, and Clifden in Co. Galway. This base was to be the first east coast wireless transmitting station.[3]

At that time, wireless telegraphy was in an embryonic stage. It would eventually bring about a total revolution in communications. Marconi was the inventor of the first successful and practical system of wireless telegraphic communication, which became a reality when he used his system to transmit the first wireless signals across the Atlantic between Poldhu and St John's, Newfoundland. The message travelled a distance of 2,100 miles in December 1901.[4] A year later, in December 1902, the first complete messages were transmitted by Marconi from stations at Glace Bay, Nova Scotia, and later from Cape Cod, Massachusetts, to Poldhu in Cornwall. The Marconi Station at Rosslare became the intermediary between Poldhu and Clifden, resulting in the opening of the first transatlantic commercial station connecting Glace Bay and Clifden via Poldhu.

Two wireless operators, brothers Charles[5] and Jack Dodd, came over from London to work with the primitive battery-operated apparatus. Messages received from shipping were taken over by hand to the post office, at that time located at Kelly's Hotel, just a short distance from the wireless station. These messages communicated the weather conditions at sea, the number of passengers on board and information for the ship's owners. The successful wireless transmitting station established by Guglielmo Marconi in Rosslare operated for thirteen years, until its closure at the outbreak of the First World

Guglielmo Marconi, inventor of wireless telegraphy.

War in 1914.[6] Rosslare had become a listening location on two occasions: first, in peacetime by Guglielmo Marconi, and then in the turbulent years of the Great War.[7]

In 1915, Rosslare entered its second phase as a 'listening zone' when the Admiralty, under the Defence of the Realm Act, took over a house named 'Four Winds'[8] on the edge of the sea at Greenore Point,[9] Rosslare Harbour. The house had been built by Lady Goulding, wife of William Goulding, chairman of the Great Southern and Western Railway (GSWR).[10] The house is situated on the edge of a high cliff with unobstructed views of the seas around the south-east coastline. Locally, the house was also known as 'White Caps', a reference to the headgear worn by the naval officers billeted there.[11]

A series of cables were laid from the house along the seabed to Tuskar Rock Lighthouse. The vibrations of the propellers of German submarines were picked up by the 'listening station' at Four Winds when they approached to lay mines. As soon as the distinctive sounds were detected by the cables, notification was sent to Rosslare Harbour, where naval vessels set out in a bid

'Four Winds', St Helen's, Kilrane, Co. Wexford. (Ann Borg)

to locate and destroy the submarines. Local man, John O'Hagan, maintained that the cable did not run directly to Tuskar Rock Lighthouse from the Four Winds house but from a stone-built hut 50 yards to the south of the actual house. The 'telegraph hut' was on the edge of the cliff and its remains were there until recent times.[12]

Rosslare played a very important role in the First World War because of its proximity to the Welsh coast and the possibility of an invasion of England by the Germans via St George's Channel and the Irish Sea. The British Admiralty placed almost fifty minesweepers in the port, to clear the area of mines, and numerous patrol boats, tasked with warding off and destroying the submarines which were becoming ever more daring and successful in their attacks on shipping.

As part of the war effort, the three Rosslare–Fishguard mail-boats were requisitioned for service as hospital ships by the British government. The vessels, *St Patrick*, *St David* and *St Andrew*, left the port of Rosslare and the cross-channel journeys were undertaken either by the SS *Great Southern* or the SS *Great Western*. These two ships were from the Waterford–Fishguard service, so the sailings from Rosslare to Fishguard were reduced to just one journey a day.

The Curragh, County Kildare, was a training camp for the British Army and during the war thousands of soldiers travelled to the war front in France via Rosslare.

Due to the presence of the German submarines in St George's Channel, the ships did not always sail between Rosslare and Fishguard, and when they did set out for Fishguard, they were accompanied by naval patrol boats. The east coast of Ireland from Antrim to Wexford was known as U-Boat Alley. During one period of the war, there was only a cargo service, which operated three times a week, carrying cargoes of bacon, butter, cream, eggs and fish. Since the onset of the First World War, mines had been laid by German submarines in St. George's Channel and the Irish Sea, causing the loss of over thirty ships and many lives around the south-east Irish coastline. Although they were frequently pursued by the U-boats, the ships of the Rosslare–Fishguard line managed to evade the undersea predators.

Some measure had to be taken to combat the danger mines posed to shipping, so in January 1915 the British government established a minesweeping base at Rosslare Harbour. Twenty-four Scottish drifters[13] and four trawlers converted into minesweepers arrived at Rosslare Port, where they were fuelled with coal delivered by steamships. Most of these minesweepers were operated by naval personnel, many of whom were in the Naval Reserve and owners of the vessels.[14]

Activity and security increased at Rosslare, with the minesweepers tied up along the pier and other destroyers and naval ships docking on occasion. Sentries were posted at all entrances to the pier and admission restricted to those with a pass enabling them to cross the viaduct.[15] At one stage, over 200 soldiers lived in tented conditions in a field on the clifftop overlooking the harbour, while the officers were billeted in local houses.

The local population was in fear of an attack by enemy craft gaining entry to the harbour and were advised by the British Admiralty to be prepared to make an immediate escape if this were to happen. These fears were allayed by the parish priest, who assured his flock that the measures were just precautionary, but fears of an invasion were renewed when the navy, conducting a regular patrol on the morning of 3 February 1915, sighted a German C409 submarine close by to Tuskar Rock Lighthouse. The patrol boat gave chase and fired ten shells at the fleeing submarine, which eluded the naval patrol boat.[16]

Several mishaps were recorded in those years off the Wexford coast, including one involving the SS *Centurion*, which had departed from its home port of Liverpool and was heading to Durban, South Africa. The ship was torpedoed by a submarine 36 miles south of the Barrels Rock Lightship, near Carnsore Point. The forty-four-man crew boarded the ship's two lifeboats in a bid to escape what they thought was their sinking ship. The ship seemed to be staying afloat, so the crew returned to the ship, but they were approached by the submarine before they could reach it and ordered to keep clear. The submarine fired another torpedo, which sank the SS *Centurion*. The crews of the lifeboats rowed the 36 miles from where their ship had sunk and eventually reached the Barrels Lightship, where they were taken on board and given food. Another Liverpool vessel, the SS *Flemish* took the men from the lightship and landed them at Rosslare Harbour. They were fed and given fresh clothing before being taken to Wexford to be cared for by the Shipwrecked Mariners Society.[17]

To avoid being attacked by the U-boats, coastal convoys assembled in Rosslare Bay and awaited naval vessels to escort them across the Irish Sea. Sometimes up to twenty ships would sail out of the bay at dusk with their accompanying naval support.

As a means of communication with incoming ships, a flagpole was erected on the clifftop, with a semaphore signalling station. Upon sighting a vessel entering the bay, the flags of the International Code of Signals were hoisted by the coastguard on duty to enquire about the name of the ship. The incoming ship hoisted her signal numbers in response and, on recognition by the coastguard, further communication was conducted using the semaphore arms.

Similar semaphore signalling was used with the minesweepers and all other naval vessels. As a means of defence, a long trench was dug along the clifftop, with outlets for rifles to be used by the soldiers manning the trench. The entire minesweeper base was under the charge of Commander Simmons.

Communication between the 'listening stations' at Four Winds, Tuskar Rock Lighthouse and Carnsore Point proved to be highly successful in detecting the whereabouts of German U-boats along this particular section of U-Boat Alley and destroying them. There were 'listening cables' situated at many points around the British Isles at this time. These were updated by the Americans. Improvements might have included the use of a loop of copper cable laid on the seabed, which would experience magnetic interference whenever a submarine passed nearby. The shore-based hydrophones had the ability to detect the motors of the U-boats, enabling them to sink them by detonating the nearby mines. Had this system been used at Tuskar, it would have been necessary to use a second 'listening station' to obtain a 'fix' on the submarine. In fact, there may have been more than one cable at Tuskar Rock Lighthouse, with the cable at Four Winds being used to detect submarines passing in the area between the lighthouse and the shore.[18] The cable at Four Winds may well have been the 'listening cable'.

Another practical use for this cable would have been to enable lighthouse keepers to transmit information on detected U-boats to the shore. The gathered information would have been relayed either by telephone or telegraph to the Admiralty station at Rosslare Harbour and from there to England. Such telegraph routes were already in existence prior to the outbreak of war. Eircom maps actually show a telegraph or telephonic link to Tuskar Rock Lighthouse.[19]

Lighthouses such as Tuskar Rock, with a cable connected to the shore, were invaluable to the Admiralty.[20] Tuskar Rock Lighthouse played a major role in the war and so it is worth giving a brief outline of its history.[21] The lighthouse is built on an islet 7 miles off the south-east tip of Ireland, measuring some 350 feet in length and 40 feet in breadth. It rises 25 feet above sea level at its highest point.[22] Prior to the construction of a lighthouse in this location, countless ships were wrecked on its jagged outlying reefs.

Eventually, following repeated requests for a lighthouse, the board of Trinity House recognised that a lighthouse was needed and work commenced in June 1812.

The workmen required for the job were recruited from St Helen's, St Margaret's and Carne.[23] The flat islet was home to twenty-four men during the building. They were housed in wooden huts fastened to steel bars that had been sunk into the rock. A sudden storm on the night of 18 October of that year resulted in the wooden structures being swept into the raging sea and the loss of ten men. The remaining fourteen men managed to survive by clinging to the Rock for forty-eight hours before they were rescued. Following their recovery, the rescued men returned to complete the construction of Tuskar Rock Lighthouse.[24]

The 110-foot-tall tower (including the balcony and lantern) began operating two years later, having cost £30,000 to build.[25] The lighthouse keepers and their families lived in dwellings at the base of the tower from 1834 until 1890, when they moved into four houses built on the mainland.

Tuskar Rock Lighthouse, aerial photograph taken in 2017. (Pat Sheridan)

The houses were occupied by lighthouse personnel and their families until 1975.

The following is a list of the lighthouse keepers at Tuskar Rock Lighthouse, from 1914 to 1918, during the First World War: John Glanville (principal keeper, 1911–16); Richard Somers (assistant keeper, 1913–17); John M. Johnson (assistant keeper, 1911–15); James McGinley (assistant keeper, 1913–18); John J. Duggan (assistant keeper, 1915–19); William J. Callaghan (principal keeper, 1916–19); Joseph D. Murphy (assistant keeper, 1917–19) and Peter Corish (assistant keeper, 1918–23).[26]

Tuskar Rock Lighthouse still stands, a sentinel of the treacherous waters around the south-eastern tip of Ireland. It played a pivotal role monitoring and tracking enemy submarines during the First World War. Together with the Four Winds and Carnsore Point, it was equipped to eavesdrop across an unobstructed 250-degree arc that stretched from the Irish Sea to the Southwestern Approaches. Working together, the three formed one of the most important U-boat observation areas in the British Isles during the First World War.[27] With the Americans stationed at Four Winds and the constant flights over the surrounding seas by planes that took off from the USN Air Base at Ferrybank, the approaches were well patrolled and protected from ravages on shipping by German submarines. Rosslare 'did listen' during those turbulent years.

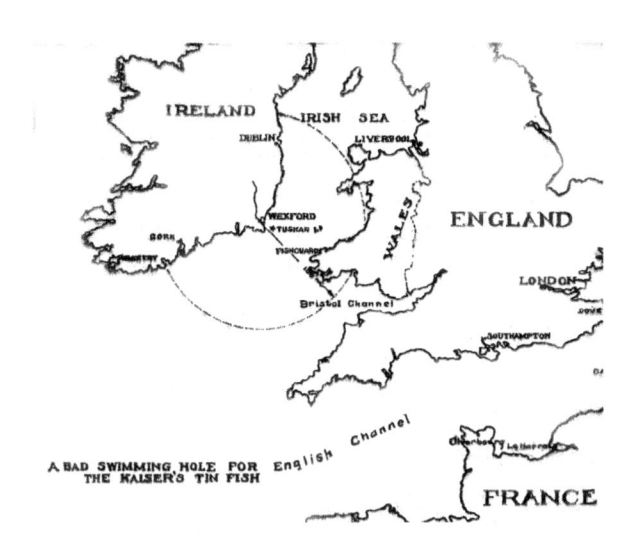

Map of flight areas by Curtiss H-16s. (Souvenir Booklet)

8

Wexford 1918

The following is a calendar of events for Wexford town and its environs in the year 1918. The information has been gleaned from newspapers – *The Free Press, The Wexford People, The Irish Independent, The Daily Mail* – and Wexford Borough Council and Wexford County Council Minute Books at Wexford County Archive, Ardcavan, Wexford.[1]

January

With Christmas of 1917 over, local business firms advertised their January sales, as they would any other January, offering all kinds of bargains in clothing, footwear, bedding, dress and curtain materials and crockery at keen prices. Barker's Earthenware Shop on South Main Street advertised earthenware, china and glass at prices that defied competition. Corry & Co. on North Main Street had a complete range of ladies' blouses, millinery and the latest dressy wear. Ladies' costumes in all modern shades were priced from 18*s* 11*d* to 5 guineas. Semi-trimmed and untrimmed hats were also available.

An article entitled 'Ferrybank Men's demands' in the *Free Press* of 12 January 1918 reported:

> On Sunday Alderman Richard Corish, Secretary of the Wexford Branch of the Irish Transport and General Workers' Union, had an interview with the contractor of the Government works at Ferrybank, where over a hundred men are employed at present. Ald. Corish demanded that the wages of the labourers be increased from 7d. per hour to 10d. and that the men be paid double time for work on Sundays. The contractor, Mr. Moran, informed Ald. Corish that

he could not settle the matter without referring the question to the Admiralty official in charge of the works, and that he would do so at once. A reply from the Admiralty is expected early next week.

ELECTION OF MAYOR ALD. MCGUIRE WINS BY BIG MAJORITY
The annual meeting of Wexford Corporation was held in the Assembly Room, Town Hall, on Wednesday 23 January at noon. The principal business was the election of Mayor for the following year. The outgoing Mayor, Mr. Nicholas Byrne presided. There was a small attendance of the general public. Alderman

Mayor William H. McGuire (1867–1940). (Padge Reck)

Sinnott proposed Alderman McGuire be elected as Wexford's Mayor. A long and heated argument ensued with other Councillors adding to the debate and eventually a ballot was held and Alderman William Hugh McGuire was elected Mayor of Wexford for 1918. Mayor McGuire served a second term of office in 1919. Born in 1867, his father, William McGuire, a ship's chandler, also served as Mayor of Wexford on three separate occasions.[2]

The following report appeared on 27 January in *The People*:

ENGLISH FOREMEN FALL-OUT
Ganger charged with Assaulting Fellow Worker
A fracas between two Englishmen employed as gangers in connection with the construction works occurred at Ferrybank on Saturday night 23 January, as a result of which one of them Joseph Thompson sustained injuries of a very severe nature. The injured man was attended at Ely House on Sunday morning by Dr.T.J. Dowse who found him suffering from a broken rib and other injuries. Thompson was removed to the County Infirmary, and as a result of information received, the police arrested Timothy Lench on a charge of assaulting his fellow-worker. In consequence of his serious condition it was deemed advisable by the authorities to take a sworn statement from Thompson.[3]

February

A naval funeral was reported on in the *Free Press* edition of Saturday, 9 February:

On Sunday 3 February the funeral of James Fox of Cornmarket, a naval reservist, took place with full naval honours. Mr. Fox, a fisherman by occupation, had joined the navy at the outbreak of war and saw active service at the Dardanelles bombardment. He had returned home in mid-summer last year in ill health and his death occurred at his home on Friday 1st. February. A respectful tribute was paid to him at his interment by the officers and men of the patrol boats who accorded James Fox a naval funeral.[4]

In an article entitled 'Strike at Seaplane Station – Men to Resume Work' in the *Free Press* on Saturday, 2 February 1918, the following was reported:

After a strike lasting four days, the labour dispute at the Admiralty Construction Works near Wexford has been satisfactorily settled. The men, numbering 180 ceased work at dinner hour on Monday, their demand for increased wages and better conditions not conceded. About a month ago, the employees, through the Transport Union, of which nearly all are members, applied for an increase of from 7d. to 10d. per hour, with double time for Sunday work. When the men's views were presented by Ald. Richard Corish to the contractor, Mr. Moran, of London, the latter intimated that he would lay the matter before the Admiralty. Subsequently the contractor expressed his willingness to increase the men's wages from 7d. to 8d. per hour and to pay time and a quarter for Sunday work. The men refused to accept 8d. per hour. They reiterated their demand for double pay for Sunday work and added that they required time and a half for work on Saturdays after one o'clock and time and a quarter for overtime between Mondays and Fridays. The contractor notified the men's representatives that he would arrive at a decision by Saturday last. Meantime, a notice was posted at the work stating that any men willing to do Sunday work would be paid time and a half, but as a protest the men refused to work for the last two Sundays. As the contractor's reply to the men's demands was not forthcoming on Saturday, the men ceased work on Monday, as stated. Negotiations between the contractor's representative, Mr. Burrell and Alderman Corish, on behalf of the men, ensued, and on Thursday evening an amiable arrangement was arrived at, the men undertaking to resume work on this Friday morning. It is stated, though not officially, that the men's demands have been granted.

Another *Free Press* article that month dealt with a very different subject matter:

Twelve years old Miss May Vize, daughter of Mr. Charles E. Vize, well-known Wexford photographer of Spawell Road has won a scholarship valued at five guineas for her performance on the violin in Grade III at the music examinations held at the Loreto Convent recently. The adjudicator predicted a career of promise for the talented young musician.[5]

A meeting of the Wexford Harbour Board regarding storage of timber on the quays was reported on at the end of the month:

'Wexford Quay', painting by Marine Artist Brian Cleare, 2017. (Brian Cleare)

The matter of timber on the quays was discussed at a meeting of Wexford Harbour Commissioners presided over by J.J. French in the presence of the Mayor, Ald. McGuire and other members of the Commissioners. A letter from the Great Southern and Western Railway Company complaining that traffic on the railway line on the quay was impeded by the timber stacked on the quayside. Various members of the Harbour Commissioners voiced their comments as to the actions of the local children throwing the timber down even when properly stacked. The Mayor maintained the timber was badly stacked and that owners of the timber were responsible. Mr. P. Donovan said a piece of pitwood was sticking out from a stack and it struck a passing train knocking off a door. Mr. J. Billington said that local merchants were paying 9d. a ton on timber storage to the Harbour Commissioners and the least the Commissioners might do was to look after it when stored on the quay. Another member requested that a watchman be appointed and to ask the police authorities to keep the children away from the timber. The consensus was to inform the Railway Company that the Board was carrying out the bye-laws and other matters on the agenda were then discussed.[6]

March

DEATH OF JOHN EDWARD REDMOND MP
Deep mourning marked the death of John Redmond
When the Irish leader, John Edward Redmond, MP, died unexpectedly in a London nursing home, Ireland was plunged into mourning, especially his loyal followers in his native Wexford. He had succumbed to heart failure after an operation.

The editorial in the local *People* newspaper stated:

Now, more than ever will the people of Ireland realise the loss that they have sustained in the death of this great Irishman. The sole ambition in his life was to win national autonomy for his country. He laboured strenuously to this end; indeed, no one can realise the terrible strain it must have been on Mr. Redmond for so long to direct the movement for attaining Home Rule. The terrible burden he had to bear, particularly of late, had so told upon his robust health that recently death was pictured in his face. And this was brought about by the treachery of those in high places whom he trusted and of a certain section of his countrymen at home who stooped to the foulest epithets to level against one who was a patriot above everything else. We refer to the small cliques of small minds who levelled the most odious charges of treachery against him, one who devoted his entire life to working so strenuously for the betterment of his country and his countrymen. That he was a thoroughly honest man and always acted for the best will be conceded by the overwhelming majority of Irishmen. As we have pointed out, the course of events for some months past has shown that even if he had pursued another line of policy, as his critics have pointed out, it is now clear that Ireland would not have been granted Home Rule in face of the opposition of Ulster.

The *Free Press* of Saturday 4 March reported on the death of the Irish leader Mr. J.E. Redmond:

DEATH OF IRISH LEADER
Mr J.E. Redmond passes away. The nation plunged into grief.
The death occurred in a London Private Nursing at 7.45 a.m. on Wednesday 6 March of John Edward Redmond, M.P., and Chairman of the Irish Parliamentary Party. Remains to be Interred in Wexford.

Mr. Redmond's remains were conveyed to Westminster Cathedral on Wednesday night where Requiem Office and High Mass, at which Cardinal Bourne presided, was held on the following day. The remains will be brought by sea to Kingstown (Dunleary) arriving on Friday night and John Edward Redmond's final journey will be by special train to Wexford on Saturday morning for burial. His remains will be accorded a public funeral in his native town. Following Solemn Requiem Office and High Mass in the Church of the Immaculate Conception, Rowe Street at 11 o'clock the dead Leader will be laid to rest in the Redmond vault in John Street Churchyard. The cortege will take the following route through School, Joseph, King, and Castlehill Streets, The Faythe, William, Parnell, Barrack, Main, Hill and John Streets. The order of the procession will be as follows – The Clergy will precede the bier, which will be surrounded by a guard of honour of the Irish National Foresters in costume. Immediately after the relatives. Members of Parliament and Convention delegates will then walk. The next place in the procession is allocated to contingents of ladies, while the Ballybricken delegates and Waterford public bodies will occupy the next sections. They will be followed by representatives of other public bodies outside of County Wexford and the County Wexford public bodies, Corporation, County Council, Urban Councils, Redmond Memorial Committee. The Committee in charge of the funeral arrangements are desirous that on Saturday morning all business should be suspended in town until after interment, and it expected that the citizens by closing business establishments and drawing blinds will pay a last tribute to the dead leader.[7]

Soon after the burial of John Edward Redmond a wreath-laying ceremony took place at the Redmond Mausoleum in St John's Graveyard, John Street, Wexford. Dr James S. Ashe, secretary of the Major Willie Redmond Memorial Committee laid a wreath on the grave of Mr John Edward Redmond, MP, in the presence of the Mayor of Wexford, William H. McGuire, and other dignitaries, including the former Mayor of Wexford, Nicholas Byrne. Also in attendance were members of the costume unit of the Thomas Moore Branch of the Irish National Foresters. The wreath was sent by the New York Municipal Council. Representing the United States of America were sailors from the USN Air Station at Ferrybank (two white-capped sailors to the left of Mayor McGuire and two other sailors behind Mayor McGuire and Dr James S. Ashe in the centre of the photograph).[8]

WEXFORD 1918

Dr. Ashe laying on the grave of Mr. John Redmond the wreath sent by the New York Municipal Council.

Mayor William McGuire with Dr Ashe at wreath-laying ceremony at Redmond Mausoleum, Wexford. American sailors present in crowd.

John Edward Redmond MP.

In an article on 'The Ferrybank Fracas', the following was reported:

At a Special court held in Waterford Jail a further remand of eight days was granted by Mr. Gerald Griffin, R.M., in the case against Timothy Lench. Mr. Lench, a ganger at Ferrybank, Wexford was charged with grievously assaulting a fellow ganger, Joseph Thompson. The assault took place at Ely House on Saturday night 23 January. Head Constable McGrath informed the court that the injured man, at present in Wexford County Infirmary, would probably be recovered enough to appear on the expiry of the eight day remand.[9]

Another article, 'The Ferrybank Fracas English Ganger Returned For Trial', read as follows:

At a special Court held in Wexford on Tuesday, before Mr John J. Kehoe J.P. presiding, Timothy Lench, a ganger at the Admiralty Seaplane Station at Ferrybank, was charged with assaulting and inflicting grievous bodily harm on Joseph Thompson, another ganger at the same works. The prisoner was conveyed from Waterford Jail, where he had been on remand since his arrest subsequent to the alleged assault. Joseph Thomson verified a deposition made by him in the County Infirmary, already published, stating that the deceased beat him on the night of the 23rd January in the mess room at Ely House, striking him five or six times and knocking him down, and subsequently punching him in the ribs. The prisoner, he stated had a grievance because he was not allowed to join the mess in which witness was. Answering the prisoner, witness said he did not wish to press the case. He denied saying that the accused might get the clothes ripped off him and denied striking accused first. Accused said they had a rough and tumble fight and added, 'E 'urt 'eeself trying to 'urt me'. Head Constable McGrath deposed to arresting the accused on the 24th ult. on a charge of breaking two of Thompson's ribs, and when charged, accused said they had been a previous row and there was bad blood since. John Breeze another English ganger, gave evidence about the row. He did not know which of the men struck first. They had two or three rounds and each of them was knocked down two or three times. Owing to the witness's unsatisfactory answering, District Inspector Patrick, R.I.C. threatened to have him committed for contempt of court. Continuing, witness said that when Thomson sat on the chair, Lench struck him four or five times, he believed, in the ribs. In answer to accused, the witness said that while Thompson was on the chair he used provoking language to Lench, and that caused the renewal of the row. Both men were sober. There was no foul play, and nothing was used but the fists. The accused pleaded to be allowed out on bail, as he had been already in jail for 16 days losing about £10 in wages. He earned £4.10 shillings to £5 a week at Ferrybank. The Prisoner was returned for trial to the Quarter Sessions, bail been fixed at £20 and two sureties of £10 each.[10]

SCHOONER SUNK
Two of crew wounded by shrapnel

The Irish schooner, 'Nanny Wignall', bound with a cargo for home was attacked on Saturday morning 16 March by a large German submarine. The U-boat was sighted a mile off heading for the sailing craft, which owing to the heavy sea running at the time, was unable to put about. The skipper, Captain Matthew O'Neill, shortened sail, but the submarine suddenly opened fire at a quarter mile range on the schooner, which was unarmed. The first shot carried away the riggings and brought down some spars. At the same time the Captain saw the boy, James O'Neill, a lad of sixteen, running along the deck covered with blood. The poor lad who was torn in the chest and stomach by shrapnel, lay down beside the wheel. The Captain abandoning the wheel ran forward to assist the other crew members to knock away the gangway and lower the ship's boat. While this operation was in progress the firing continued uninterruptedly, and seaman Laurence Smith was struck by a piece of shrapnel in the ear. The skipper and the mate, Pat Pender, and seaman Matt Neill succeeded in rescuing their wounded comrades under a hail of fire which brought the sail, spars and masts tumbling down on the deck. The submarine did not cease the murderous

Wexford Courthouse. (Lawrence Collection, National Library of Ireland)

'Tug and Sailing Ships at Wexford Quay', painting by Brian Cleare, 2017. (Brian Cleare)

fire until the ship's boat was well clear of the vessel. She followed the crew in their tiny craft and the captain believed at the time that the Germans meant to finish them, but when two hundred yards off, the submarine returned to the schooner and sank her by shell-fire. After a perilous journey in a stormy sea, the crew, who had been six hours in an open boat, reached land. Young O'Neill was conveyed to the County Infirmary, where he lies in a critical condition. This latest outrage by the submarines has caused the greatest indignation locally.

The People newspaper made an important announcement, entitled 'Increase in the Price of Our Papers':

Owing to the further drastic restrictions imposed by the Government on the Paper Supply and the great increase in the expenses of newspaper production we have found it necessary to increase the prices of Saturday issues of our newspapers from 1½d. each copy to 2d. each copy. Accordingly beginning with our issues of April 6th. and until further notice the Price of 'The People' (Saturday's 'New Ross Standard', 'Enniscorthy Guardian' and 'Wicklow People') will be 2d. each copy.

April

In the Wexford Notes for the 6 April issue of the *Free Press*, the following appeal was printed:

ST BRIGID'S BAND
The well-known Wexford musical combination, St. Brigid's Fife and Drum Band has been recently reorganised and an effort is being made to restore the band to its former high standard. In order to achieve this, it has been found necessary to procure new instruments as well as to renovate older ones and the committee would be glad if friends would show their appreciation of the services of the band by helping them in their difficulty. It is to be hoped that the deserving appeal will meet with a generous response.

In the issue of the *Free Press* dated Saturday 27 April 1918, the following report appeared:

ARMS RAIDS IN WEXFORD
Police Seize Traders Stocks

During the week the premises of the various merchants in town who trade in sporting arms and ammunition were entered by the police who, under the authority of the Defence of the Realm Act, took possession of firearms and explosives. On Tuesday morning the hardware establishment of Mr. James J. Stafford, M.C.C., was visited by the police in charge of Sergeant Collopy, and the stock of sporting rifles, cartridges etc. on the premises were seized. On the following day a party of police under the command of Head Constable McGrath, searched the premises of the following traders – Messrs. Healy's, Hamilton's, Joseph Murphy, Robert Coffey and Matthew Harpur, and took possession and commandeered their stocks of guns and explosives. The seized stocks were removed to the Military Barracks, Wexford. On Wednesday, a motor car in charge of two armed policemen arrived in Wexford with a quantity of sporting arms which had been taken possession of in the Gorey District.

May

FIGHT WITH A SUBMARINE
Sunday Morning Scene Off Irish Coast

Sunday's quiet in an Irish seaside resort was unduly disturbed when gun-firing began a short distance from the shore, and soon vantage points were crowded with eager listeners, who were rewarded by witnessing a rare duel between an enemy U-boat firing from the shelter of a thick belt of haze and a small three-masted coasting cargo steamer, only a few hundred yards from the shore. It was at once evident that the latter was making a heroic effort for life by brisk movement and rapid reply to the enemy shooting. For over twenty minutes the struggle, unequal as it necessarily was, continued with ever-increasing interest for the people onshore. The cargo boat, admirably handled by her captain and crew, turned towards port, zigzagging continuously, and sending forth a dense smoke screen. This, however, was wafted shorewards by the breeze, which, unfortunately, favoured the submarine at the time. Shells fell thick and fast around the steamer, each one raising a great cloud of spray. None of them, however, struck their object, some soaring over her, but the majority falling short. The German gunners must have been poor marksmen. Making for harbour, the steamer kept up her splendid reply to the enemy, and the onlookers could distinctly see the spray thrown up by her shells, but the

German Navy U (Unterzeeboot) Boat U.20 which operated off the Wexford and Waterford coasts.

U-boat 20. (Duncannon Archive. Co. Wexford)

submarine did not come within view. Eventually the firing ceased, and the little steamer glided safely into the shelter of the harbour, amid great cheering.[11]

June

Major William Hoey Kearney Redmond was the brother of John Edward Redmond and also served as a Parnellite MP for East Clare, a seat he retained until his death in 1917. Major Redmond died in action in Flanders on 7 June 1917 and is buried at Loker (Locre), Dranoutre, Belgium. Preparations had begun early in 1918 for a commemorative ceremony in Wexford town. A fund had been initiated to raise money for a memorial to be erected in Redmond's honour, with the Lord Lieutenant of Ireland as patron and Dr James S. Ashe as honorary secretary. Lady Maurice Fitzgerald of Johnstown Castle was Ladies' President of the Wexford committee.

In the 'Wexford Notes' in the *Free Press* on 15 June, the following account appeared:

> Another labour dispute, but which fortunately was of a brief duration, occurred at the Admiralty Construction Works at Ferrybank this week. On Tuesday evening at four o'clock sixty carpenters engaged on the construction of a hangar, for which Messrs Thompson Brothers, Wexford, are contractors, ceased work on the grounds that two of their fellow-workers had been dismissed without notice, and had not been given their railway fare to their homes. As the railway fares are advanced to the men when employed by the Labour Exchange

Major William Redmond MP (1861–1917), Chevalier de la Légion d'honneur.

for such work, they claimed that their fares home when their services are being dispensed with, should also be defrayed by their employers. The dispute spread on the following day when labourers to the number of sixty or seventy, who had been engaged to attend the American Naval Carpenters 'downed tools'. On the carpenters marching to the works in a body to procure their tools they were denied admittance until noon, and were only allowed in at that hour in batches of a dozen accompanied by an armed escort. Meanwhile sentries with fixed bayonets were posted about the works, and a strong force of armed police under District Inspector Patrick was also in the vicinity. There was no disturbance, however, and matters passed off quietly. Shortly afterwards Mr. Thomas McDermott, Irish Organiser of the Carpenters' and Joiners' Society, and Mr. Thomas Walsh, the local Secretary of the Union, interviewed the contractor, the Admiralty Engineer and the US Naval Commander at Ferrybank and an amicable arrangement was arrived at, the demand of the men being readily acceded to. The strikers resumed work on Thursday morning.

'Soldiers and Sailors Concert':

The usual fortnightly concert for the soldiers and sailors was held on Monday in the Town Hall, and it was perhaps the most enjoyable function that has been held so far in the town for a long time. By kind permission of Lieutenant Mason it was given by the men stationed at Fourwinds, Kilrane, and was under the capable management of Chief Petty Officer Davies, who was accompanist for the evening, as well as giving musical monologues and performing some clever imitations on the piano. The programme was varied and the different items were received with applause by a large audience present. The opening item was a quartette, 'Four Jolly Sailor Men' and during the evening several concerted pieces were rendered. Recitations were given by C.P.O. Bourne. Solos by C.P. Officers Henderson, Shaw, Gladston, Mason and Mrs. Brown. Duets from well-known comic operas were given by C.P.O. Shaw, Davies and by Miss Sylvia Richards. Rev. Mr. McMullan, on behalf of the committee returned thanks to those who had contributed to so delightful an entertainment, and especially to C.P.O. Davies, the organiser.

July

At a meeting of Wexford Borough Council on 1 July 1918 the Mayor W.H. McGuire; Aldermen Sinnott, Corish and Carty; and Councillors Lymbery, McMahon, Gibson, Keating and Kirwan were present. The meeting concluded with the following greeting:

The following Resolution was unanimously adopted on the motion of Alderman Carty and seconded by Councillor David R. Keating: 'That we, the Wexford Corporation, representing the people of Wexford, wish to join with the Americans in our midst in celebrating the one hundred and forty-second Anniversary of the Declaration of America's Independence on July 4th. That a copy of this Resolution be forwarded to the Commander of the U.S. Sea-Plane Station at Ferrybank.'[12]

CASTLEBRIDGE FAIR

At the monthly fair held at Castlebridge on Thursday there was a fairly large supply of cattle on offer, which sold at latest rates. Three-year-olds brought from £35 to £40; two-year-olds from £25 to £30; and yearlings from £13 to £16. Beef, of which there was a limited supply, sold well. In other departments there was a somewhat meagre supply of stock, prices ruling pretty high.

ADMIRALTY DREDGING

At a meeting of the Wexford Harbour Commissioners, a letter was read from the Secretary to the Commander-in-Chief, the Coast of Ireland, as follows: – 'The superintending civil engineer reports that your Harbour Board Commissioners have informed him that they cannot allow any more of the material being dredged near the Wexford Seaplane Station to be dumped in Cull Channel. In your letter of the 18 June, 1918, you informed us that your Commissioners gave authority to deposit dredged material in Cull Channel, which had been used by the Board for this purpose for the past fifty or sixty years. The remaining dredging to be done is comparatively small, and a great delay to the work would ensue if dredged material had to be taken over the bar into the harbour. The Commissioner-in-Chief requests that your Commissioners will continue the permission to be allowed to deposit material in Cull Channel until the completion of the work now in hand'.

On the suggestion of the Chairman of the Wexford Harbour Commissioners it was decided to allow the dredged material to be dumped in Cull Channel when the weather did not permit the barges to cross the bar, and to notify the authorities to this effect with an intimation that the Harbour Commissioners expected that in favourable weather, the dredged material should be dumped outside the harbour.[13]

August

'Decorated' – *The Free Press*, 3 August 1918:

Two of the officers attached to the Flying Station at Johnstown Castle have just returned there from London, where they were decorated by the King. Captain John Eld. Barres received the Distinguished Service Cross for his 'heroic and successful action with a submarine last December'. The operator who accompanied him, namely, Mr. A. M. Tattershall, and who was in charge of the gun and the wireless at the time, received the Distinguished Service Medal. We heartily congratulate Captain Barres and Mr. Tattershall upon their gallantry and the honours they have so well earned.

WEXFORD HARBOUR BOARD
At a meeting of the Wexford Harbour Board, the Secretary reported that in regard to the proposal to extend the abutment of the old bridge at Ferrybank he stated that the Board had been in communication with the Board of Trade

Air balloon at mooring station, Johnstown Castle, Co. Wexford. (Irish Agricultural Museum Archive)

and the Commander, USN Air Forces, had informed him that the project had been sanctioned by the Admiralty. The Chairman stated it was a question for the Board whether they would be bound by the Admiralty or make an appeal to the Board of Trade. This work could not be carried out without the permission of the Board of Trade and the Harbour Board. The Admiralty had no right to give permission as the pier was the property of the Harbour Board, who had been paying for it for years and should not allow the USN Air Forces the exclusive right to it without being paid for it. This matter should be put in the hands of their solicitors which was opposed as it might lead to a costly lawsuit. The Mayor agreed and said when the Admiralty had power to take possession of public roads in the district and had given no compensation they could do the same thing with the abutment. The Chairman said if the project was required in connection with the war, neither the Board of Trade or the Admiralty would come to the Board's assistance. It was decided to take no action in this matter.

AWARDED A MEDAL
William O'Leary, son of Mrs. O'Leary, Michael Street, Wexford, has been awarded a medal by the Admiralty for gallantry at sea.

During the month of August, there was industrial unrest at two of Wexford's manufacturing firms. 'Pipe-Maker's Wages' made the following report:

A demand for increased wages by the men employed at the Wexford Pipe Factory was granted by Messrs. Murphy Bros., proprietors of the factory. The firm agreed to increase the wage paid to pipe-makers from 1s. to 1s 4d. per gross manufactured. The labourers employed by the factory be paid a minimum wage of 30s. per week.

Messrs. Murphy decided to compare the rate of wages paid to labourers in a similar concern in Waterford and in due course Alderman Richard Corish, Secretary of the Transport Workers' Union, was negotiating on behalf of the Wexford staff communicated with the secretary of the Waterford Branch of the Trade Union outlining the wage increase demand. The Waterford firm agreed to the demand and when this course of action was adopted Messrs. Murphy Brothers offered the terms stated above which were accepted.

Similarly, 'Strike at the Star Ironworks' noted a second instance of such unrest:

Star Iron Works, Wexford. (Hearn Collection)

A strike involving almost fifty moulders occurred at the Star Ironworks, Wexford on Friday last. The cause of the strike germinated from the workmen being dismissed for refusal to obey orders. With the introduction of some new work being introduced there was a dispute as to the rate of pay per piece completed. Pending the adjustment, a time worker was given the work to do. On his refusal to carry out the work he was dismissed resulting in the rest of the moulders ceasing work as a protest and leaving the work they were involved in as a protest. The work was left in an unfinished condition. A deputation from the local branch of the Iron Founders' Union are expecting to meet with Mr Thorpe, Manager of the Star Ironworkers to discuss the disagreement. This meeting took place on Friday 30 August. The men on strike agreed to discuss the price being paid for the new work but management contended that the dispute was not a question of wages, but a matter of principle. Mr. C. Farrelly, President of the Dublin Branch of the Ironfounders' Society visited Wexford and interviewed the men. With Mr. Byrne, the Secretary of the Wexford Branch, Mr. Farrelly went to the Star Ironworks and met with management which brought a settlement to the dispute with the men resuming work on the terms offered by the firm.[14]

September

Entertainment at the Theatre Royal

The following three advertisements appeared in the *Free Press* on the following dates as separate items announcing entertainments coming to the Theatre Royal, Wexford, during September 1918:

9 September: Michael E. Fitzgerald and His Club Juggling Girls performed for 6 nights at the popular Wexford venue. The Fitzgerald show included Violet MacKinnon Ireland's celebrated blind pianist and mezzo-soprano, Tom Quain, baritone, supported by a big company of Vaudeville Artistes.

20 September: Walter McNally, famous operatic baritone presented his Concert and Operatic Recital with Kathleen McCully, soprano; Florrie Ryan, contralto; Lucy Leenane, pianist; Rosalind Dowse, violinist; Harry O'Dempsey, tenor; Annie Sande, Irish dancer and Power and Bendon, comedians.

The programme 'Gems from the Operas' featured excerpts from 'Faust'; 'Maritana'; 'Il Trovatore'; 'The Lily of Killarney' and 'The Bohemian Girl'. Admission prices were Boxes 2s.4d., Pit Stalls 1s.10d., Pit 1s.3d., Gallery 8d. Doors open 7.30 p.m., Curtain 8 o'clock.

30 September: For one week only, Barry's Music Hall and Variety Company with a galaxy of stars including the 5 Barry Sisters, the only Lady Acrobats touring Ireland appeared at the Theatre Royal to packed houses.

ADMIRALTY DREDGING

At a recent special meeting held on the 21 September of the Wexford Harbour Commissioners concerning dredging work being carried out by the Admiralty, the Chairman gave details of a conversation he had with Mr. Hilderbrand, Admiralty Engineer. On the question of allowing the dredged material to be dumped in the deep hole in the river opposite the slipway at Ferrybank it was pointed out to Mr. Hilderbrand that such permission that was sought would be a great advantage to the Admiralty and the Harbour Commissioners would be entitled to a substantial sum of money for granting this application. At the special meeting it was decided that Mr. Hilderbrand be informed that the Board were prepared to allow the dredged material to be dumped on the whole on the condition that the Harbour Commissioners receive a sum of £2,000. It was necessary that the Commissioners in view of their unsatisfactory financial position should take such steps to protect themselves against the considerable damage that would be likely to occur to the berths and harbour. In reply to the Chairman, the Secretary said he had not received any communication since from the Admiralty.[15]

October

An advertisement announced, 'The most economical way to increase tillage is by using – "STAR" ploughs and Spring Tooth Harrows all manufactured by the Wexford Engineering Co. Ltd. and sold by M. Hearn & Son, New Ross.'

Another advertisement read, 'For Artificial Teeth please Consult Mr. J. D. Quinn, Dental Surgery, 73 North Main Street, Wexford. Mr. Quinn supplies Highest Grade Artificial teeth, Guaranteed for Comfort, Durability and Natural Appearance at very moderate charges. Teeth extracted without the least Pain.'

In the *Free Press* for the 5 October 1918, this article on the decoration of the Captain and Crew of the South Arklow Ship was headed and reported as follows:

WEXFORD LIGHTSHIPMEN HONOURED
DECORATION FOR CAPTAIN & CREW OF THE SOUTH ARKLOW SHIP
For Signal Services to Shipping.
Submarine Commander's Revenge Recalled.
During the week Captain James Rossiter, The Faythe, Wexford, Master of the South Arklow Lightship, was notified that the King had been pleased to award to him and the crew of the South Arklow Lightship 'The Torpedo Badge', a special distinction created to denote that the wearer had performed exceptional services to shipping at the risk of his own life. The distinction, which was only recently created, is being conferred on Captain Rossiter and his crew, all of whom are Wexfordmen, for services rendered as far back as March, 1917, when they risked their lives in the performance of their duty, in warning mariners of the presence of danger. Their action on that occasion, however, differed from their everyday avocation of appraising seamen of the perils which beset their path along the Arklow coast, for the danger they heralded was not one

which nature has placed there in the shape of rugged rocks or shifting sands, or capricious currents, but a menace of human device which lay lurking in the shelter of the shoal awaiting its prey. A submarine had been lurking near the lightship all day and sunk the little schooner, 'Harvest Home' of Wexford, outbound across the channel. The Captain and crew looked on helplessly at this disaster and the fate of the crew of the schooner. On the approach of another vessel the lightship signalled to warn of the presence of the submarine. The merchantman put about and escaped the German attack. The merchantman in turn warned other vessels in the Channel of the impending danger thus the vigilance of Captain Rossiter and his crew it was estimated that at least 20,000 tons of shipping was saved. The German submarine now turned on the lightship ordering the crew to abandon ship and take to the boats. Bombs were placed on the lightship and leaving the crew adrift in an open boat the submarine made off returning later when all was clear and shelled the lightship, sinking her. Captain Rossiter and his men were eventually picked up by the 'Anman' a steamer from Glasgow. The Captain and all hands from the South Arklow Lightship were landed safely the next day in Wicklow. The crew members were awarded this distinction and certificates testifying to their action were:- Patrick Cogley, School Street, Martin Murphy, King Street, John Leader, Green Street, Peter Gaddren, The Faythe, all from Wexford town. The other crew members were – Patrick Sinnott and James Sinnott from Courtown, County Wexford. This incident occurred in March 1917.

November

Stephen Doyle wishes to announce he has recently taken over the business at 66 South Main Street where he will supply the very best quality in Bacon, Hams, Lard, Cod and Ling Fish.

Thomas Buckland, 50 South Main Street specialises in the sales of Tobaccos, Cigars, Cigarettes, Pouches and other smokers requisites. Buckland's also carry a first class range of Fountain Pens with such makes as The Swan, The Cameron and The Waterman. Other makes also kept in stock.

CASTLEBRIDGE DISPUTE
Messrs. Nunn, Malsters, Castlebridge, having given a week's notice to their employees in consequence of the refusal of the latter to deal with corn which

had been handled by the non-Union men, Very Rev. Canon Quigley P.P., convened a meeting of the men on Friday last, and the latter agreed to deal with all corn at the stores. Alderman Richard Corish having previously advised them to do so for this reason. Intimation to this effect having been conveyed to Mr. J. L. Nunn, the latter, on receiving a personal assurance from his employees individually, that they would handle all corn withdrew the notices of dismissal which were due to expire on Saturday and work is proceeding in the firm as usual.[16]

A FAVOURABLE RECORD
During the week Sergeant Michael Collopy, South Main Street, Wexford was notified by the Inspector General, R.I.C. that he had been granted a third class favourable record and monetary award in efficient police duties. Sergeant Collopy had been commended by the Wexford Magistrates for his efforts in bringing to justice the perpetrators of numerous larcenies in the town and district, the successful prosecutions since he took charge of the station involving no less than fifty-one offenders. The Inspector General expressed his appreciation of the sergeant's successful efforts to put down crime in the district.[17]

December

In the issue of the *Free Press* for Saturday 7 December, one of the items addressed by Wexford Corporation was the contents of a letter received from Mr Barry, Wexford Gas Consumers, on the situation regarding street lighting in the town and was reported as follows:

THE PUBLIC LIGHTING
The principal business before the meeting of Wexford Corporation was to take steps to have the public lighting of the town improved.

Mr C. Barry, sec. pro tem, Wexford Gas Consumers Co; had written that, 'the number of lamps lighting after dark was 61 on the town and 9 on the quays. After a short time the full 115 would be lighted as last year.' He added that, 'the Company, were keeping an account of the numbers, and of the dates when lamps were put up'. Regarding the complaints of the heavy smell from the gas, he said, 'it was owing to the purifiers not working properly, but these had been rectified, and he felt sure the Corporation would have no further cause of complaint'. The Town Clerk, Mr W.A. Browne, said, 'the Corporation had temporarily appointed Mr N.J. Cosgrave as lighting inspector to ascertain how many lamps were lighted by the Gas Company. The Inspector's report tallied with the statement of the Gas Co. that 70 lamps had been lighted, though on the one occasion the number was down to 65.' The Mayor said that 'the Gas Company's letter was satisfactory'. He hoped the Company would soon be able to fulfil their promise to light the 115 lamps.[18]

DEATH OF THE HISTORIAN OF '98

Father P.F. Kavanagh, O.F.M. passes away while at prayer. The death of the historian of the Insurrection of 1798 took place at the Friary in Wexford on Tuesday morning 17 December as reported in the Free Press of Saturday 21 December. The venerable Franciscan was engaged at prayer in his humble cell when called to his eternal reward. The unexpected death of the cleric was a sad event for the people of his native town causing deep grief in all those who knew him.[19]

Fr Patrick Kavanagh, OFM, historian.

WEXFORD 1918

The following notice appeared in the *Free Press* in December 1918:

> Wanted – 4,000 Turkeys, Geese, Chickens etc. for Xmas Markets. prices offered; Turkeys, Geese, Chickens, Ducks and Old Fowls all at 1 shilling per pound. All bought at live weight daily at James Boyle, John's Gate Street, Wexford.

The final year of the Great War ended with the celebration of Christmas and the hope of a new beginning, with the onset of another year.

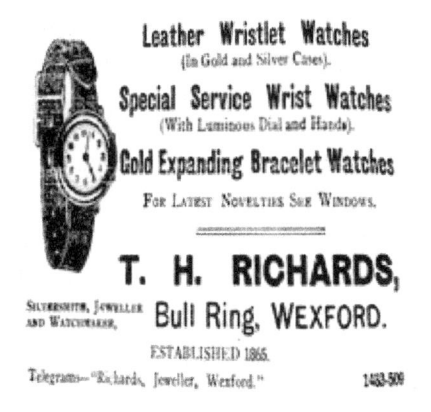

Free Press advertisements 1918.

9

War Is Over

World War One came to an end with a ceasefire starting on the eleventh hour of the eleventh day of the eleventh month 1918, bringing to an end four battle-filled years on land, sea and skies across Europe. The Compiègne Armistice was signed, with drastic terms imposed on Germany, during a meeting in a railway carriage of Marshall Ferdinand Foch's private train deep in the Forest of Compiègne in the Picardy region of France. On Monday, 11 November, the Press Bureau issued the thirty-four conditions of the Armistice subject to a specific time limit of acceptance or rejection within seventy-two hours of their issue. The duration of the Armistice was to be thirty-six days, with the option to extend. During this period, on failure of execution of any of the clauses, the armistice may be denounced by one of the contracting parties on forty-eight hours' previous notice.

Peace would return once again with members of the armed forces coming home again to loved ones and families. The news of the armistice was particularly well received in Wexford with the announcement of the cessation of war. The *Free Press*, in its issue for Saturday, 16 November, carried the following heading:

ARMISTICE SIGNED.
DRASTIC TERMS
IMPOSED
Official Text of the Terms

The newspaper published the thirty-four conditions of the armistice in detail numbered from 1-34. The following terms were set down by the Allied powers for the Armistice:

'The conditions to become effective within six hours after signing. The immediate clearing of Belgium, France, Alsace-Lorraine within 14 days with any troops remaining in those areas to be interned or taken prisoners of war. The surrender of armaments including 5000 cannon, 30,000 machine guns, 3000 trench mortars and 2000 planes.

Complete evacuation of the left bank of the Rhine, Mayence, Coblence, Cologne which were occupied by the enemy. Evacuation of the right bank of the Rhine forming a neutral zone of 30 to 40 kilometres wide, within 11 days. All factories and railways on the left bank of the Rhine to be left intact and the surrender of 5000 locomotives and 150,000 railway carriages and 10,000 trucks. The Treaties of Brest-Litovsk and Bucharest to be renounced and the unconditional surrender of East Africa. The property of the Belgian Bank, Russian and Rumanian gold and all prisoners of war to be returned'.

With the involvement of the British Admiralty and USN Air Stations in Ireland, in particular in Wexford, combating the havoc and loss of life to naval and merchant shipping by the German submarines the author of this work has given particular notice to Armistice conditions from No. 20 upwards.

Regarding Naval Conditions, the *Free Press* reported as follows:

Condition No. 20 – Immediate cessation of all hostilities at sea and definite information to be given as to the location and movements of all German ships. Notifications to be given to neutrals that freedom of naval and mercantile marines of the Allied and Associated Powers with all questions of neutrality being waived.

No. 21 – All naval and mercantile marine prisoners of war of the Allied and Associated Powers in German hands to be returned without reciprocity.

THE SUBMARINES
No. 22 – Handing over to the Allies and United States of all submarines (including all submarine cruisers and mine-layers) which are at present at the moment with full complement in the ports specified by the Allies and the United States; those that cannot put to sea to be deprived of crews and supplies, and shall remain under the supervision of the Allies and the United States.

Submarines ready to put to sea shall be prepared to leave German ports immediately on receipt of wireless order to sail to the port of surrender; the remainder to follow as early as possible. The conditions of this article shall be carried within fourteen days after the signing of the Armistice.

THE SURFACE SHIPS

No. 23 – The following German surface warships shall be designated by the Allies and the United States of America shall forthwith be disarmed and thereafter interned in neutral ports, or, failing them, Allied ports to be designated by the Allies and the United States of America, and placed under the surveillance of the Allies and the United States of America.

Listed were: Six Battle Cruisers; Ten Battleships; Eight Light Cruisers, including 2 Mine-layers and Fifty destroyers of the most modern types.

All other surface warships including river craft are to be concentrated in German naval bases to be designated by the Allies and the United States of America, and are to be paid off and completely disarmed and placed under the supervision of the Allies and the United States of America. All vessels of the auxiliary fleet such as trawlers, motor vessels etc. are to be disarmed. All vessels specified for internment shall be ready to leave German ports seven days after the signing of the Armistice. Directions of the voyage will be given by wireless.

No. 24 – The Allies and the United States of America should have the right to sweep up all mine-fields and obstructions laid by Germans outside German territorial waters, and the positions of these are to indicated.

No. 25 – Freedom of access to and from the Baltic to be given to the naval and mercantile marines of the Allied and Associated Powers. To secure this the Allies and the United States of America shall be empowered to occupy all German ports, fortifications, batteries and defence works of all kinds in all entrances from the Kattegat into the Baltic, and to sweep up all mines and obstructions within and without German territorial waters, without any questions of neutrality being raised, and the positions of all such mines and obstructions are to be indicated.

BLOCKADE MAINTAINED

No. 26 – The existing blockade conditions set up by the Allied and Associated Powers are to remain unchanged, and all German merchant ships found at sea are to remain liable to capture. The Allies and the United States of America contemplate provisioning Germany during the Armistice, as shall be found necessary.

No. 27 – All German aircraft are to be concentrated and immobilised in German bases to be specified by the Allies and the United States of America.

No. 28 – In evacuating the Belgian coasts and ports, Germany shall abandon all merchant ships, tugs, lighters, cranes and all other harbour materials for inland navigation, all aircraft, materials and stores, and all arms and armaments and all stores and apparatus of all kinds.

Conditions Nos 29, 30 and 31 pertain to Russia's warships of all descriptions seized by the Germans in the Black Sea which are to be handed over to the Allies and the United States of America and all merchant ships in German hands belonging to the Allied and Associated Powers are to be restored in ports to be specified without reciprocity. No destruction of ships or materials was to be permitted before evacuation, surrender or restoration:

MERCHANT SHIPPING
No. 32 – The German Government shall formally notify the neutral Governments of the world, and particularly the Governments of Norway, Sweden, Denmark and Holland, that all restrictions placed on the trading of their vessels with the Allied and Associated countries, whether by the German Government or by German private interests, and whether in return for specific concessions, such as the export of shipbuilding materials or not, are immediately cancelled.

The penultimate condition of the Armistice (No. 33) brings to a conclusion the conditions with the exception of No. 34, which outlined the duration and limitations of the Armistice as already mentioned at the outset of this chapter.

No. 33 – No transfer of German merchant shipping of any description to any neutral flag are to take place after the signature of the Armistice.

This report brought an air of calm to the citizens of the town and its environs, in particular those many local sailors and naval personnel whose lives were

Admiral Sir David Beatty, Royal Navy.

endangered on a daily basis in maritime pursuits. The seas around the south-east coast of county Wexford would be safe once again from the vicious attacks on and destruction of merchant and naval shipping by the dreaded U-boats of the German Navy. It was a County Wexford-born naval officer, Admiral David Beatty, who accepted the surrender of the German Navy thus bringing to an end all war at sea.[1]

The declaration of the Armistice resulted in a wave of celebrations across European counties occupied by the enemy. In County Wexford, celebrations occurred across the four county towns where families waited expectantly for the safe return of loved ones who had participated in the four-year war, serving in the armed services.

On Monday evening, enthusiastic demonstrations took place in Wexford town. Tar barrels burned in several parts of John Street; Rowe Street; Old Pound; The Faythe; Maudlintown; William Street; Anne Street; the Bull Ring; at the Redmond Monument; the Ballast Bank; Talbot Street and Bride Street. The Bride Street Fife and Drum Band turned out and a procession was formed and marched through the principal streets, cheering for the Allies, the Royal Irish and the Irish Brigade. The procession paused at the Knights Templar churchyard in John Street, where they cheered loudly for John E. Redmond and Major Willie Redmond. After the cheers subsided, prayers were quietly recited for the late Irish leader, John E. Redmond. The celebrations continued into Tuesday night, particularly in Bride Street. This street had given so many men to the fighting forces, many of whom never returned from the battlefields of France and Belgium. Tar barrels blazed again during the night.

During that week, Masses were celebrated in Taghmon, Castlebridge, Mulrankin, Piercestown and Ballymurn for the repose of the souls of all fighting men from the county.

Enniscorthy also welcomed the Armistice with great celebration. On Tuesday night, bells were rung at St Mary's Protestant church to mark the joyful news and prayers were recited at St Aidan's Cathedral in thanksgiving. The welcome news was heralded in Gorey with the ringing of the Joy Bells of Christ Church. Tar barrels blazed and rockets lit up the night sky.

Many of those who enlisted did not return home to Wexford town and the surrounding areas. They died in places such as the Dardanelles and the muddy, rat infested trenches of Northern France and Belgium. It is estimated that between 27,000 to 55,000 Irishmen died in the First World War, 500 of them from County Wexford.

The following are some of the men from Wexford town who died:[113] Philip Barker, Rowe St; Patrick and Richard Berry, (brothers) Bride St; Thomas Berry; Patrick Bolger; Joseph Boyce; Peter Boyle, Bride St; John Breen; Joseph Breen, Bride St; Myles Brennan; Edward Breslin, Rowe St; John Brien; William Brien, Rowe St; William Broaders; James Browne; Robert P. Browne; Edward Busher; Peter Byrne; Thomas Byrne, Rowe St; Joseph Carley; John Carthy; Patrick Cleary; Murtha Clowery; John Coady; Patrick Collins; Michael Cosgrove; Michael Curran, Bride St; Michael Dempsey, Bride St; William Devereux, Rowe St; John Fanning; Michael Farrell; Peter Farrell; Martin Fenlon; Gerald Hugh Fitzgerald, Johnstown Castle; John Furlong, Rowe St; James Hall, Rowe St; Nicholas Hatchell; Patrick Holbrook; John James; Thomas Kearns; William Leacy; Thomas Lawlor, Rowe St; William Moore, Bride St; James C. Murphy, Bride St; Matthew Murphy, Bride St; James O'Connor, King St; James Redmond, The Faythe; Joseph Roche, Maudlintown; Patrick. Roche, Rowe St; William Roche, Rowe St; Patrick Ryan, Bride St; Nicholas Sane, Rowe St; John Saunders; John and Richard Sherwood (brothers), Parnell St; Patrick Whitty, Bride St.

It is obvious that soldiers from Rowe Street and Bride Street made a major contribution to the war effort in answering the call to arms by John Edward Redmond, paying with their lives. Many families were depleted and deprived of their breadwinners.

An article entitled 'Wexford Doctors Fear an Epidemic – Vital need for Vaccination' warned of the smallpox that had come in the wake of previous wars:

> As epidemics of small-pox have invariably followed the great wars of the past the prospect of the termination of the present conflict the gigantic nature of which but increases the danger of a similar tragic aftermath renders it imperative on those charged with the care of the public health to consider seriously and at once the terrible possibility of an outbreak of plague and to take full and adequate steps to safeguard their charge. The best known preventative of small-pox is vaccination, and though differences of opinion may exist as to the justice of the Vaccination Acts, as they apply to this country, and even as to the efficacy of vaccination itself, the consensus of public opinion and the practically unanimous opinion of the medical profession warrant us in regarding vaccination as the most reliable and effective precaution to take against an outbreak of this loathsome disease. For some years past compliance with the Vaccination Law has been more or less neglected with the result

that there are today in the country thousands of children who have not been afforded the protection that vaccination would give them in the event of such an epidemic. The need for immediate action in this matter is obvious, and in view of the public attention that is bound to be centred on the question within the next few months, the opinions of local medical practitioners will be of interest to those, who in the fog of the controversy to form a judgement in the matter. Our local doctors, all of whom agreed as to the efficacy of vaccination. Doctors Thomas Pierce, T.J. Dowse, S.V. O'Connor and James Ryan all agreed that vaccination was imperative for the protection of our children and adults alike. The consensus of the local doctors maintained that vaccination would be a preventative of small-pox, and the objections against it are very few and can often be avoided by due care in the selection of the source of the vaccine and in the operation of vaccination, at the same time making sure that the patient is fit and healthy.

Wexford town did have an outbreak of influenza in epidemic proportions. In the course of a week, the virus spread at an alarming rate, as reported by the *Free Press* in the issue of 5 November 1918:

The Sanitary Officer said that there were cases of the 'flu in practically every street in town, estimated at over 200 cases, and all the medical practitioners are busily engaged attending the patients, whose numbers are increasing daily. Many of the cases of 'flu are described as 'very serious'. In at least two cases those stricken with this malady have died. One of the victims was Mr. Mitten, efficient sub-postmaster at Wexford General Post Office whose death is deeply regretted. Elaborate precautions are being taken in all local factories and workshops by way of disinfection. All the local doctors are requesting that all schools be closed in the town. At a meeting of Wexford Corporation acting on the suggestion of their sanitary officers have called for the immediate closing of all schools immediately. The Corporation also recommended the closing of the local picture houses. Three cases of typhus fever have also occurred in town within the past month.

Eventually Wexford town began to return to normality as peace settled once again over the area, and its citizens set their eyes on the not-too-distant festive season and what it might bring.

10

Out of Sight

Secrecy regarding the arrival of USN forces at Ferrybank was crucial and so there was no local press coverage of the event. Nothing of the American war activities at Ferrybank was ever broadcast at a national level either. For security reasons, the written accounts of life at the air station are very sparse, except for the letters of Chester McNichol. He described some of the social activities he and others were involved in during their stay. Visitations to Wexford town and its environs are mentioned, in particular dances, films and bars in the town and the many 'local' activities within the confines of the air station, such as football, baseball, boxing and concerts at the YMCA.

Many friendships were forged with residents of the town, especially with the female population, resulting in several marriages. One such marriage took place between Elizabeth Delaney, a native of Francis Street, Wexford, and Glow B. Philips, a radio electrician, 1st class, who served at the USN Air Station, Ferrybank. On his return home to the United States, following the Armistice, Glow Philips, who had formed a relationship with Elizabeth, wrote to her parents in Wexford seeking her hand in marriage. Following some correspondence between Wexford and America, permission was granted for a marriage to take place in the United States. The young 18-year-old Wexford girl set out for the 'New World' in a passenger ship bound for New York. On landing safely in that huge city, she had to journey across America to the West Coast and her final destination of San Diego, where her husband-to-be was stationed. They duly married and became the parents of two boys and one girl. Over the decades, visits were made between Ireland and America, to see cousins and in particular to return to Francis Street, the home place of Elizabeth Delaney.[1]

The 'Yanks' were warmly welcomed during the short months they spent in Wexford, when they built, occupied and operated the USN Air Station at Ferrybank 100 years ago. Aside from the series of nine available letters, Chester McNichol also sent letters from several other locations on his journey back home to the United States, including Dublin, Cork, Liverpool and New York. The Wexford letters cover a period from April to the end of November, 1918, and are an important record as they give an insight into life for the occupants of the air station.

Chester J. McNichol was born in Arlington, Middlesex, Massachusetts, in October 1891. Both of his parents were Irish-born. Following the entry of America into the First World War, Chester McNichol's completed draft card showed his occupation as a chauffeur. He was 26 years old when he was appointed to serve at the USN Air Station, Ferrybank, in 1918. He is listed in the crew roll list as 'Ship's Cook, 1st Class' and was in Ferrybank from the arrival of the US Navy personnel earlier that year. At the end of the war he left the station, moving to Dublin, Cork, Liverpool and back to America via France. His last residence was Bellows Falls, Windham, Vermont, where he died in March 1982 in his 90th year. During his stay in Europe, he corresponded with his friend, William Toomey at 85 Beacon Street, Arlington, Massachusetts, from all of the locations. Nine letters in total were written from Wexford and were of a friendly nature, with no information relating to the activities of the USN Air Station at Ferrybank.

The first letter in this series to his friend William (Bill) Toomey is dated Wednesday, 24 April 1918, and it mentions that Chester had been transferred just eighteen days ago to another place (Wexford) since he had last written to Bill.

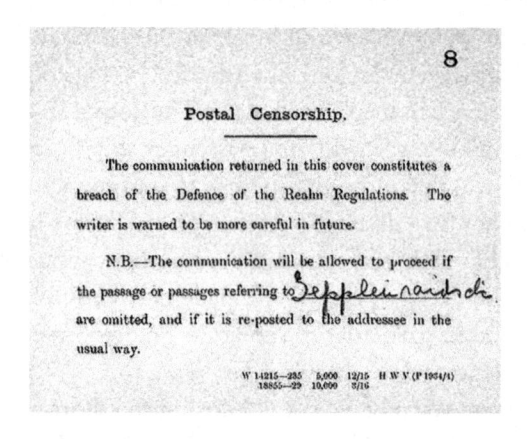

Postal censorship notice, First World War.

McNichol is a ship's cook and there is no shortage of food available both to cook and to eat. He describes the scene in which the station is located, with green pastures, hedges, cows and sheep. As he says, 'it is some pretty country'. With summer coming, he thinks it will be a little warmer and there will not be so much rain. He closes this letter with good wishes to all the folks and hopes that Bill in a return letter will give him a little news about the happenings in his village back home.

A letter written on Sunday, 19 May 1918, reads: 'certainly glad to hear from you', as it is in response to a letter from Bill, and he tells him that his mail is always welcome. He goes on, 'We get liberty nights and Sundays but as the car service is not like home, we find it very hard to get places we would like to visit. This afternoon there is a ball game in the field. Things are running about the same as when I wrote last.'[2]

In a letter of Sunday, 9 June 1918 to Bill Toomey, Chester states: 'the new Y.M.C.A. Hall on the air station was opened last week. There was singing and music from some of the crew at the premises. On the previous night I went to the movies and they were pretty good. Next week's film is *Darina*.' Chester closes his letter with a report on the local weather and a request for Bill to write soon.

A letter of Sunday, 14 July 1918 to Bill Toomey, Chester enquires about the weather back home. 'Well, tell Gert for me that I hope she will have the best of luck and that she will meet with success in anything she may undertake. Please thank her for her recent letter, which I will answer soon. Hoping you, Ma and Da and the rest are in good health, as I am myself. Chet.'

In a letter written on Friday, 16 August 1918, Chester writes:

> That's some surprise you put over on me. I mean that box of candy. I want to thank you very much, as it was very nice. Yesterday, I went to a beach, about four miles out. Two hotels, three bars and a grocery store were the only attractions there, although the sand was very fine and lots of pretty shells.[3] About a week ago I went to a horse race, the jockeys wore all colours and some were pretty fast. Fakirs were also there giving fortunes away. I think in a few days we will have movies on the station here. As it is, we have to go over to town, which I do very often. The Fourth was quiet here, having a few games and a big feed.[4]

It is obvious from the tone of Chester's letter dated Monday, 7 October 1918, that Bill had taken offence as he had not received a letter from him for over two months. Chester refuted this accusation, saying that he had replied to him. Maybe the letter had gone astray in the mail? The next part of his letter makes for interesting reading:

> One afternoon about a week ago, two of us volunteered to go in a motor truck into the country picking apples. We landed in an orchard near a farmhouse. The trees were very low, so they came pretty good. While we were thus engaged, the farmer and the rest of the family brought out some fresh butter, a pitcher of milk and a large oval loaf of wheat bread. It was all very plain, but it was the real stuff. One of the sailors that hails from Somerville said it reminded him of the time he used to be on the road. On 3 October, one of the fellows that works with me got married to a girl from Liverpool. His home town is Elgin, Illinois. It was a surprise to us, but next day we got over it and gave them a nice silver tea-set. Now look after your Ma and Gert. Nothing else, I think, of any interest. Chet.

In his letter of Friday, 1 November 1918, Chester addresses Bill as William – very formal. The letter is worth quoting:

> Today like a lot of others we are having now, is rainy. It isn't well to venture out unless we have a raincoat with us. Wednesday afternoon, a young fellow, another sailor and myself walked out to a place called Edenvale.[5] One hour and a half each way. Believe me it was some pretty too. One of those big waterwheels, turned by a falls – they use it to grind wheat. Everything around it was green, being in the woods about a mile.
>
> In coming back, we stood in the road and looked down in a valley covered with small brush and trees. Right in the centre was one of those thatched-roof houses and another smaller one, both were whitewashed on the outside. About four cows were grazing and lying about the place, also a couple of donkeys and their carts, while in another corner three goats were munching away, making it a perfect picture. I only wish I had my canvas and brushes with me.
>
> Last Saturday afternoon, another sailor and I went to that fellow's house that got married of which I spoke in the last letter, and had tea with him and his wife. About eight o'clock, we went to the first Yankee dance held in the burgh (borough), it took place in the town-hall with our own orchestra from the station supplying the music.[6] I had a few dances with this sailor's wife. We had a right good time. The colleens don't dance like we do, so I expect we will have a little trouble in showing them our way.

Edenvale Waterfall, Castlebridge, Co. Wexford. (Charles E. Vize, colour tinted by William Ritchie and Sons, Printers, Edinburgh)

So the landlord at 63[7] gets just as dizzy as ever? There are some salts here that take too much ginger ale, and we have more fun than a barrel of monkeys. Bill, I didn't scratch that photo, it was done by Mr. Vize. I think I could have done it better myself.

You ask me why I don't visit Cork? We aren't allowed to go there. It used to be that about ten fellows could go to Dublin over Sunday but now that's stopped. So we just go to places near the station. I would certainly like to look this place Ballincollig over, get pictures of it and when I get back tell your grandfather about some of the changes that have taken place. I have just taken out a $100 Liberty Bond on this South Drive, ten to be taken out of my pay each month. Some took $50, $100 and $200. About $23,000 was realized. About a fortnight back, I was made Ship's Cook, First Class. Now I hope you are satisfied that you know where I fit.

He then signed off.

His final letter from Wexford, dated Thursday, 28 November 1918, opens with a bit of stage Irishism:

The top of the afternoon to you, William,

Today, Thanksgiving, like a lot of others is gloomy as this country seems to be noted for its (soft) weather. It begins to get dark shortly after four o'clock in the afternoon and keeps thusly until eight the next morning. Believe me, it's some darkness too. I can't work out how some of these salts get back to the station after they get tanked up over town. I used to lead a few of them back, but lately I'm off that stuff and get back a little earlier and don't meet them as often. In the morning, there was a football game between Queenstown and Wexford, the former winning. In the afternoon, a Minstrel Show is pulled off in the Y.M.C.A. and is pretty good. We have a dance on for the night. It is taking place at Kelly's Hotel at a sort of summer resort and seashore place called Rosslare.[8]

We start about eight o'clock, two girls and an elderly lady (their aunt) as chaperone, as I'm told that it's the custom here. A chief pharmacist and myself are also in the party, he being the one that got this all together. We use the station ambulance to go down in. After lounging around the hotel for a while, we start dancing about ten o'clock. There's a few that can dance a little but more that can't, so when I had gone around for a while I got a kink in my arm. About eleven-thirty, we had a light banquet after which we danced some more. It's nearing 4am when we are about to start back again. Everyone had been drinking more or less including this guy I'm with, excepting the ladies. He does the driving with his girl by his side and this lady and another girl with me. We are inside in the fliver [American slang for rundown car] about the same build as N. K. Hutchinson's. The night is dark and the roads narrow and not a house within forty miles I don't think.

Well, sir, when we were about a mile from the hotel, instead of taking a turn in the road our driver keeps straight ahead and the next thing we know we are in the ditch. He said it was alright, that he could pull it out and he didn't. So, after working around it about half an hour, I suggested lifting the rear end right up and placing it near the road, which he did. Then I got in it and backed it up on dry land. When it first landed it was tipped like the roof on a house.

The rest of the trip was without any other mishap, arriving about five o'clock, left the lady folks off and got at the station about five-thirty, had breakfast, changed clothes and started to work. Such was the end of a perfect day. There's a fellow that lives in Somerville who went out of here a couple of days ago and said he would go out to my house and tell the folks that I was alright. He's one of those happy-go-luckys, been on the stage and has a good voice. He is a hard-looking character, rough in manner and talk, but not as hard

ROSSLARE HOTEL.

PROMENADE ROOF.

TENNIS & CROQUET.

POST AND TELEGRAPH OFFICE ATTACHED TO HOTEL.   MARCONI WIRELESS TELEGRAPH STATION WITHIN ONE MINUTE'S WALK OF HOTEL.

This New Hotel, Three Storeys High, which is built on the beautiful Strand of Rosslare, is unrivalled for its

POSITION, COMFORT, AND MODERATE CHARGES

And having a Promenade Roof, commands a fine view of Bay and Rosslare Harbour and surrounding Districts.

HOT AND COLD SEA AND FRESH WATER BATHS.

THE PUBLIC RESTAURANT & TEA ROOMS

Adjoining the Hotel are the Largest in the South of Ireland.
TEAS supplied from 6d. each
Hot and Cold LUNCHEONS supplied on Shortest Notice.

W J. KELLY, Proprietor.

Advertisement for Kelly's Hotel, Rosslare, Co. Wexford. (Bill Kelly)

THANKSGIVING DAY
1918.

MINSTREL SHOW.

— UNITED STATES — NAVAL AIR STATION, WEXFORD, IRELAND.

Minstrel Show, Thanksgiving Day 1918, USN Air Station, Wexford. (Dermot McCarthy)

Selection of sheet music covers of songs performed at Minstrel Show.
(L. Gaul)

as he looks. I suppose I will spend Christmas on this side, if I do I'm going to try and keep away from dances.

Well Bill, there isn't much more. So wishing the whole bunch a Merry Christmas and Happy New Year will bring this to a close. Love, Chet.

McNichol's eighth letter is transcribed in Chapter 4.

Thanksgiving Day menu cover 1918. Farewell Dance programme and menu, Kelly's Hotel, Rosslare, 27 February 1919. (Bill Kelly)

Bill of Fare at Kelly's for US Naval Airmen

Enclosed with the final letter Chester wrote while in Wexford was the printed programme of the abovementioned Minstrel Show held at the Station to commemorate Thanksgiving Day 1918. The show was comprised of selections of popular songs of the time, all performed by personnel from the air station, and was an American form of entertainment developed in the early nineteenth century. Such shows consisted of comic skits, variety acts, dancing and music, with the entire programme introduced by an interlocutor aided and abetted by first and second 'End Men' and 'Middle Men'.

The opening number was 'N'everything', followed by the nostalgic 'Wonderful Mother of Mine' and other titles such as 'We Don't Want the Bacon'; 'Don't Slam That Door'; 'Dear Old Pal'; 'Land of Wedding Bells'; 'Oh! How I Hate to Get Up'; 'Ship of My Dreams'; 'When Uncle Joe Steps Into France'; 'Wait 'Till the Cows Come Home'; 'Asleep in the Deep'; 'Rock-a-by Baby'; 'Love's Lullaby'; 'Rose of No Man's Land'; 'My Old New Jersey Home' and 'When Irish Eyes Are Smilin'. Banjo and violin selections were also part of the show, with a grand finale of 'Old Glory Goes Marching On'. The overall tone of the music and song featured was very patriotic, as suggested by the music titles. Twenty men from several different departments at the station participated throughout the programme. The border on the cover of the programme was a rather strange one as it was comprised of lots of swastikas.

For security reasons, all US Military mail was subject to censorship at this time. The envelopes which contained the letters from McNichol during those months show signs of having been examined by the station censor in Wexford and a British civilian censor, who would have added a censor tape to the envelope. The Wexford censor stamped the envelope with the A-15 cancel number. The British censor's examination most likely occurred in Liverpool, from where American military mail was usually dispatched.

This important and informative series of letters has been transcribed with the permission of the owner of the letters.

'Letters from Home', line drawing from USN Souvenir Book.

'Thoughts of Home', line drawing from USN Souvenir Book.

11

The Yankee Slip
The Aftermath

The buildings at the USN Air Base were dismantled and advertisements appeared on the front page of the *Wexford People* newspaper on 3 and 17 May 1919 announcing the sale by auction of valuable items from the base. The sale was handled by the Belfast auctioneering firm of Messrs Gray and MacDowell. The contents of the auction included almost new portable buildings, jetty piers, seaplane hangar sheds, water and other storage tanks, boats, 20 tons of caustic soda, 2 tons of Ferro silicon, 50 tons of new oak and pitch pine planks and scantlings, 20 tons of loose corrugated iron, piping installation, nine steel-built seaplane lighters, derricks, bricks, cement and other materials, telegraph and scaffolding poles, metal scrap, wireless receiving towers and miscellaneous arisings. In conjunction with the Ferrybank auction, similar auctions were held at the other USN Air Bases at Queenstown (Aghada) and Bantry (Whiddy Island). Castletown-Bere and Berehaven were also included in the Bantry sale.

The Wexford auction was very successful, with practically all of the property being disposed of at high prices. The two hangar sheds were sold to an Irish firm at 925 guineas each and five petrol tanks were bought at £130 each by a Queenstown firm. The pier extension was purchased in trust by some members of the Wexford Harbour Commissioners at £200. This agreement to purchase had been sanctioned by the commissioners at a meeting prior to the auction taking place. Some seaplane lighters were purchased at £110 each by buyers from Dublin. Water gallon tanks were also disposed of at prices ranging from £200 to £260. Mr James J. Stafford, MCC, bought some

SALES BY AUCTION.

W. P. GRAY AND McDOWELL, LTD.

UNITED STATES NAVAL AVIATION STATIONS, IRELAND.

IMPORTANT DISMANTLEMENT SALES BY AUCTION

OF THE COMPLETE VALUABLE ALMOST NEW PORTABLE BUILDINGS, JETTY PIERS, SEAPLANE HANGARSHEDS, WATER AND OTHER STORAGE TANKS, BOATS, 20 TONS CAUSTIC SODA, TWO TONS FERRO SILICON, 50 TONS NEW OAK AND P. PINE PLANKS AND SCANTLINGS, 20 TONS LOOSE CORRUGATED IRON PIPING INSTALLATION, NINE STEEL BUILT SEAPLANE LIGHTERS, DERRICKS, BRICK, CEMENT, AND OTHER MATERIALS, TELEGRAPH AND SCAFFOLDING POLES, METAL SCRAP, WIRELESS RECEIVING TOWERS, AND MISCELLANEOUS ARISINGS.

TO BE SOLD BY AUCTION.-
AT
WEXFORD, CO. WEXFORD,
ON
TUESDAY, 20th MAY.

DESCRIPTIVE CATALOGUES, giving full information, price 2s. each, may be had from Commanding Officer U. S. Naval Aviation Stations (Ireland), 15 Sackville Street, Dublin; Officer in Charge at Aghada and Wexford Stations; Town Clerk, Bantry; or

W. P. GRAY AND MACDOWELL, LTD.,
AUCTIONEERS AND VALUERS,
40, CHICHESTER ST., BELFAST.

Wires: "Realise, Belfast." 'Phone 99.
(e2751-4)

'USN – Sales by Auction', advertisement in Wexford *Free Press*, May 1919.

---

electric wiring and the Enniscorthy Co-operative Society made purchases amounting to £1,050.

There were many talented men among those who served at Ferrybank, who were musicians, singers, athletes, boxers and even poets. One such lyricist was Gordon E. James, a carpenter's mate, 1st class, who penned quite a lengthy poem entitled 'The Story'. His poem tells the tale of the building of the air station, with all its toil and turmoil, from the lack of proper waterproof clothing and boots to protect the workers against the inclement Irish weather to the daily chores and work the men were expected to do from dawn to dusk. Gordon E. James concludes 'The Story' with this final verse:

And now I'm through the telling, I hear a chorus swelling,
A victory chorus for the boys who won; The spirit of a nation,
Was true of WEXFORD Station, So let the tale so stand – of work well done.

Prior to the departure of the officers and men of the US Naval Air Station in Wexford, the following short speech was delivered to them by Commander Victor D. Herbster:

You have worked long and hard, and have responded gladly and willingly to every duty. You have been eager to sacrifice; you have given a wonderful exhibition of loyalty, fidelity and obedience. For your unswerving devotion to duty, for your touching loyalty and for your hearty co-operation, – I thank you.

We have all been proud of our station, and I am glad and proud to have served with you. I wish each and every one of you happiness and success. Do not lose the Wexford Spirit, keep alive Navy Ideals, and remember whether awake or asleep the Wexford motto – 'Results Count'.

In the years following the departure of the American servicemen, very little happened in the vicinity of the former air station. The slipway became covered with seaweed as the tide ebbed and flowed over the concrete slab. This once prohibited area had been reclaimed by the local townspeople as a place to walk on fine summer evenings. Anglers cast their lines into the waters, hoping for the silvery reward of a fish dangling from a hook, its

USN Air Station at Ferrybank viewed from the air, 1918.
(USN Souvenir Book)

scales reflecting in the sunlight. At low tide, a narrow strip of sand appeared, forming a short strand where young children paddled in the sea under the careful watch of parents glad to have an opportunity to avail of the weather as the happy shouts of delighted youngsters carried across the waters. At times, local fishermen hauled their boats onto the slipway to carry out repairs or to apply anti-fouling to their craft. All memories of flying boats taking off and landing on the tranquil waters of Wexford Harbour were forgotten as the decades passed. The sight of an airplane on the Yankee Slip was never again to be repeated – or was it?

Twenty-one years later, in 1939, just prior to the onset of the Second World War, there was an airplane on the slipway once again. On this occasion, the airplane was towed onto the slipway, unable to take off due to engine failure and a damaged wing.

On Friday afternoon, 3 March, three Vickers Supermarine Type Walrus Is amphibians, N18; N19; and N20, purchased for the Irish Army Air Corps, set off from Southampton to Baldonnell Aerodrome.[1] Due to bad weather conditions, only one of the planes, N19, reached Baldonnell. The N20 diverted to Milford Haven and the N18 developed engine trouble in the vicinity of Carnsore and made a forced landing in the sea near 'Whelkeen' Rock. The sea was high and visibility was very bad. The Kilmore Lifeboat was notified and cruised in the vicinity of the Rock, but failed to locate anything unusual. In the meantime, the airplane drifted towards the shore and the crew of two landed on the beach after a most exciting and dangerous experience. The local residents began to assemble with a view to offering assistance. A tractor, belonging to Raymond Doyle of Broadway and driven by Patrick Kehoe of Bennettstown, was called into action in an attempt to save the aircraft from the water. Were it not for this and the help given by Coxswain Thomas Ryan, several members of the Carne life-saving crew, who provided additional tackle, and the local Civic Guards and other willing helpers, it is more than probable that the airplane would have been battered to pieces in the mountainous surf.

After a night's work in the piercing cold, the tractor brought the airship to safety. On close inspection, it was discovered that the damage was confined to one of the floats and a battered wing. All day Sunday, large crowds gathered to admire the beautiful aircraft and hopefully to witness the airplane take to the skies again following some repairs. The damage was too bad to allow this to happen.

The Rosslare Harbour Lifeboat, the *KECF*,[2] arrived on the scene on Sunday evening and after a series of flashes, the aircraft's take-off was postponed until Monday morning, when the airplane taxied from Ballytrent to Wexford, a distance of about 12 or 13 miles along the surface of the water.

Lieutenants Higgins and Quinlan, who had piloted the craft when it landed, were again in charge. The Rosslare Harbour Lifeboat, commanded by Coxswain James Wickham, accompanied the airplane to its new moorings. The airplane was moored in the centre of the River Slaney, in readiness to be taken to the old Yankee Slipway at Ferrybank, and if repairs were impracticable, the 'plane would be dismantled and removed to Baldonnell Airport'. When the airplane arrived at Wexford, the quayside was quickly thronged with sightseers, while many people eager for a close-up rowed out in small boats. Throughout the day, the aircraft was the centre of much

Supermarine Walrus No. 20 on the sea at Killiney, Co. Dublin, 1939–40. (Irish Air Corps Museum)

THE YANKEE SLIP

interest, particularly amongst the schoolboys, who were greatly excited at the nearness of such a warlike craft.[3]

The 17-foot-high seaplane passed through the village of Castlebridge a few days later, having been partially dismantled and loaded onto a tractor and trailer. It was taken by road to Dublin and finally to Baldonnell Airport. The sight of a seaplane going through the village caused great excitement and wonder and was the main topic of conversation for days afterwards.[4] The Walrus seaplane was the last aircraft to rest on the Yankee Slipway.[5] This is the same Walrus that is on exhibition in the Fleet Air Arm Museum at Yeovilton in the UK.

Since the end of the Second World War in 1945, the slipway has served only as a location to repair, paint and apply anti-foul paint[6] to small fishing and pleasure boats plying the waters in and around Wexford Harbour. One of the last sailing craft to 'sit' on the slipway was a refurbished river barge, *Knocknagow*, owned by Richard Miller from Shortalstown. The original length of the barge was reduced by 6.5 feet to enable her to use the entire Grand Canal system by 'cutting' and re-welding both parts together again. Luckily there was a watertight bulkhead at the after end of the hold, so the bit removed was from the hold. All that needed to be done then was to float the stern end on the next tide and bring all together again. All this work was carried out on the slipway at Ferrybank. Richard was assisted in this monumental task by his friend Jim Kiely. The completed barge, in its 'new' form, was launched once more into the waters of the River Slaney at Ferrybank.

Knocknagow river barge on Yankee Slipway at Ferrybank, Wexford. (Rossiter Collection)

The *Knocknagow* is a century-old barge that spent most of its working life ferrying goods on the River Suir. The diesel-powered barge was formerly owned by the Dowley family of Carrick-on-Suir and transported goods on the tidal part of the Suir between Waterford and Carrick-on-Suir for much of its working life. It was too big to transport cargo on the difficult stretch of the river from Carrick-on-Suir to Clonmel. The *Knocknagow* would have towed barges as well as transporting its own cargo on the Suir. After its time in Carrick-on-Suir, the barge was used by Roadstone to dredge the bed of the River Slaney for some years. To get her from Carrick-on-Suir, the normal crew brought her to Duncannon, where a seagoing crew took control. She had a large air bottle to start the engine. This allowed for two starts. The inexperienced crew used up both without success. She was in the way of fishing boats wanting to go to sea. One boat gave her a tow to go to anchor. The captain managed to put her in gear and she started, due

The Yankee Slip at Ferrybank, Wexford, 2017. (Gaul Collection)

to her 48-inch propeller, then it was all go to Wexford. The barge was saved from dereliction by Richard Miller, who restored her. He used the barge solely for pleasure and made many cruises up the River Slaney and down the south-east coastline to Kilmore and the Hook, even on to Crosshaven in Cork and travelled many times to the River Shannon via the Grand Canal. Eventually Mr Miller sold the barge to the Goggin family in 2004 and they carried out further restoration. They now use it as a pleasure boat on the River Shannon.

It is now over fourteen years since any use has been made of the slipway, with the exception of the occasional pleasure craft being hauled up for repairs on the slipway. It is obvious from the photograph that it is gradually being covered by seaweed and the flotsam and jetsam washed up by the tides. The opening entrance wall to the slipway has been closed off in the last two years in the interest of safety and as a possible barrier to rising tidal

Aerial view of slipway showing garage and hospital, 2017. (Pat Sheridan)

waters, which in winter storms lead to flooding of the main road leading to Castlebridge.

To commemorate the centenary of the USN Air Station occupancy at Ferrybank, Wexford County Council intend to develop a sunken garden with interpretive display boards at the site of the pier jutting into the tranquil waters adjacent to the slipway, which aims to make visitors aware of the history of aviation and the presence of the American Navy at the site during the First World War.

The Yankee Slipway was witness to so much activity, albeit for just a few weeks in 1918, when American aviators flew off into the skies in search of enemy submarines. We should remember the officers and crews and, in particular, the seaplanes which operated from the waters of Wexford Harbour.

Sunset over Wexford from the USN Air Base at Ferrybank. (PatSheridan)

Bibliography

Alan Aherne (ed.), *A Wexford Century – 100 Years in 100 Pages. Millennium Supplement*, Wexford: People Newspapers, 1999.

Breen, Gerry (ed.), *Rosslare in History*, Rosslare, County Wexford: Rosslare Historical Society, 2016.

Cowley, Robert, and Geoffrey Parker (eds), *The Reader's Companion to Military History*, Boston, USA, 1996.

Coy, L., B. Cleare, J. Boyce and B. Boyce, *Rosslare Harbour*, Dublin, 2008.

Culleton, Dr Edward, *On Our Own Ground, Vol. 1*, Wexford: Wexford County Council Public Library Services, 2013.

Fitzgerald, Pat, *Down Paths of Gold: A Portrait of Cork Harbour's Southern Shore*, Cork: Litho Press Co., 1992.

Forde, Rev. Walter (ed.), *The Castlebridge Story*, Castlebridge: Kara Publications, 2009.

Furlong, Nicholas, and John Hayes, *County Wexford in the Rare Oul' Times: Co. Wexford 1910–1924, Vol. IV*, Wexford, 2005.

Gahan, John V., *The Secular Priests of the Diocese of Ferns*, France: Editions du Signe, 2000.

Gaul, Liam, *A Window on the Past*, Wexford: self-published, 2012.

Hayes, T., K. Hurley, W. Roche and N. Rossiter (eds), *A Wexford Miscellany*, Wexford: Wexford History Publications, 1994.

Hayes, T., K. Hurley, W. Roche and N. Rossiter (eds), *Walk Wexford Ways*, Wexford, 1988.

Jenkins, James, *Retailing in Wexford, 1930–1990*, Enniscorthy, County Wexford.

Kehoe, Mary T., *Wexford Town – its Streets and People*, Wexford, 1985.

Kelly, Bill and Vonnie, and Ronan Foster (comp.), *The Book of Kelly's*, Dublin, 1995.

Leach, Nicholas, *The Lifeboats of Rosslare Harbour and Wexford*, Dublin, 2007.
Lewis, Kevin, *What the Doctor Ordered*, Nonsuch, 2008.
Long, Bill, *Bright Light, White Water: The story of Irish lighthouses and their people*, Dublin, 1993.
Maddock, John, *Rosslare Harbour: Past and Present*, Dublin, 1986.
Maddock, John, *Rosslare Harbour Sea and Ships*, Harbour Publications, 1996.
O'Leary, Jack, and Nicky Rossiter, *Maritime Wexford – The Life of an Irish Port Town*, The History Press Ireland, 2014.
O'Sullivan, Dr Austin M., and Peter Miller (in association), *Putting Ireland on Four Wheels*, Enniscorthy, 2014.
Power, John, *A Maritime History of County Wexford, Vol. II 1911–1960*, Kilmore Quay, Co. Wexford: Olinda Publications, 2011.
Rafferty, Celestine (comp.), *Between Place and Parish*, Wexford: Wexford County Council Public Library Service, 2004.
Reck, Padge, *Wexford – A Municipal History*, Wexford, 1987.
Rossiter, Nicholas, *My Wexford*, Dublin: Nonsuch Publishing, 2006.
Rossiter, Nicholas, *Wexford, a history, a tour and a miscellany*, Dublin: Nonsuch Publishing, 2005.
Rowe, David, and Christopher Wilson, (eds), *High Skies – Low Lands – An Anthology of the Wexford Slobs and Harbour*, Enniscorthy, 1996.
Rowe, David, and Eithne Scallan, *Some Houses of Wexford*, County Clare: Ballinakilla Press, 2004.
Stokes, Roy, *U-BOAT ALLEY: The U-Boat War in the Irish Channel during World War I*, Gorey, Co. Wexford: Compuwreck, 2004.
Tillotson, C.B., C.E. Riley and G.E. James, *US Naval Air Station, 1 Jan. 1919*, Peckham, London, 1919.
Walsh, Dan, *100 Wexford Country Houses – an illustrated history*, Enniscorthy, 1996.
Walsh, Nellie, *Tuppences Were for Sundays: Reminiscences of a Life*, Wexford, 1996.

BIBLIOGRAPHY

Newspapers

Daily Mail
The Free Press
Irish Examiner
Irish Independent
The Wexford People

Periodicals

Crofton, Monica, 'Wexford Town and "The Great War" 1914–1918', *The Bridge Magazine*, No. 32, 2014, Enniscorthy.
McCarthy, Dermot, 'US Naval Air Station, Wexford, 1918: the McNichol letters', *Journal of the Bannow Historical Society*, Wexford: 2008.
Rossiter, Nicholas, 'Sixty Five Years Ago in Castlebridge', *The Bridge Magazine*, Vol. 8, No. 2, 2004, Enniscorthy.
Rossiter, Nicholas, 'Bridges That Took Us Over the Water', *The Bridge Magazine*, Vol. 9, No. 2, 2005, Enniscorthy.
Rossiter, Nicholas, 'When America "Invaded" Castlebridge', *The Bridge Magazine*, No. 29, 2011, Enniscorthy.
Tunney, Dr. Hubert, 'The U.S. Navy in Castlebridge Parish in the First World War – 1918', *The Bridge Magazine*, No. 34, 2014, Enniscorthy.

Pamphlet

Murphy, Celestine (ed.), *Wexford Connections – The Redmond Family and National Politics*, Wexford County Council Public Library Service, September 2014.

Journals

Journal of Bannow Historical Society, No. 1, 2008.
Journal of Rosslare Historical Society, No. 5, 2016.
Journal of Taghmon Historical Society, No. 3, 1999.
Journal of Wexford Historical Society, No. 21, 2006–07.

Wexford County Archive

Wexford Borough Council (formerly Wexford Corporation) minutes, WX/CORP/1/6 (1917–29).
Wexford County Council minutes, WXCC/1/7 (1916–20).

Websites

http://www.bbc.co.uk/timelines/zp9x39
http://www.biography.com
http://www.britannica.com/biography/reinhard-sheer
http://www.centenialoffflight.gov/essay/aerospace/curtiss/Aero2.htm
http://www.history.com/topics/us-presidents/woodrow-wilson
http://www.history.com/topics/kaiser-willhelm-ii
http://www.historylearningsite.co.uk
http://www.firstworldwar.com/atoz/qships.htm
http://www.firstworldwar.com/bio/house.htm
http://www.firstworldwar.com/bio/jellicoe.htm
http://www.firstworldwar.com/bio/tirpitz.htm
http://www.militaryfactory.com
http://www.nationalpubliclibrary.org

Notes

Introduction

1 Tincone – '*Tigh an Chuain*' translates as 'the house of the harbour'. It is in the civil parish of Ardcolm in the Barony of Shelmaliere in the Wexford Union. The District Electoral Division (DED) is Ardcavan, with the Ordnance Survey (OS) number 37. (Celestine Murphy (ed.), *Between Place and Parish*, Wexford County Council Public Library Service, 2004, p. 88.)
2 *Tuppences Were for Sundays*, Nellie Walsh, self-published, 1996, p. 1.
3 Nellie Walsh (1913–97) was born in Wexford and lived there until her death in 1997. Possessed of a wonderful contralto voice, Nellie was the first voice heard in Balfe's opera, *The Rose of Castile*, which was performed at the first Wexford Festival of Opera and the Arts in 1951. Nellie sang the role of Louisa, the innkeeper. She continued as a chorister every year up to her retirement from the stage at the close of 1992 opera season. She was also a collector and singer of Irish folk songs and ballads, many of which she recorded for HMV records. Nellie was awarded an LLCM (Licentiate of the London College of Music) in 1973 at the age of 60. Her brother was Dr Thomas J. Walsh, one of the founders in 1951 and the first Artistic Director of the now internationally acclaimed Wexford Festival Opera. (Kevin Lewis (comp. and ed.), *What the Doctor Ordered*, Dublin: Nonsuch Publishing, 2008. p. 241.)

Chapter 1

1. Franz Ferdinand Carl Ludwig Joseph Maria was an Archduke of Austria-Este, Austro-Hungarian and Royal Prince of Hungary and of Bohemia and, from 1896 until his death, heir presumptive to the Austro-Hungarian throne. In 1900, Ferdinand gave up his children's rights to the throne in order to marry a lady-in-waiting. While in power, he attempted to restore Austro-Russian relations while maintaining an alliance with Germany. In 1914, a Serb nationalist assassinated him. One month later, Austria declared war on Serbia and the First World War began. Born 18 December 1863 in Graz, Austria, he was assassinated on 28 June 1914 at Sarajevo. (http://www.biography.com.)
2. The Black Hand movement wanted Serbia to be free from Austro-Hungarian rule. The movement was founded by Captain Dragutin Dimitrijevi, better known as 'Apis'. Gavrilo Princip, the assassin of Franz Ferdinand and his wife Sophie at Sarajevo on 28 June 1914, was a member of the Black Hand movement. (C.N. Trueman, 'The Black Hand Movement', *The History Learning Site*, http://historylearningsite.co.uk.)
3. Thomas Woodrow Wilson (1856–1924), the twenty-eighth US president, served in office from 1913 to 1921 and led America through the First World War (1914–18). An advocate of democracy and world peace, Wilson is often ranked by historians as one of the nation's greatest presidents. Wilson was a college professor, a university president and a Democratic governor of New Jersey before taking up residence in the White House in 1912. Wilson tried to keep the United States neutral during the First World War, but ultimately called on Congress to declare war on Germany in 1917. After the war, he helped negotiate a peace treaty that included a plan for the League of Nations. Although the Senate rejected US membership in the league, Wilson received the Nobel Prize for his peace-making efforts. Born on 28 December 1856 in Staunton, Virginia, he died on 3 February 1924 in Washington, DC. (http://www.history.com/topics/us-presidents/woodrow-wilson.)
4. US Army General John J. Pershing (1860–1948) commanded the American Expeditionary Force (AEF) in Europe during the First

World War. The president and first captain of the West Point class of 1886, he served in the Spanish- and Philippine-American Wars and was tasked with leading a punitive raid against the Mexican revolutionary Pancho Villa. In 1917, President Woodrow Wilson selected Pershing to command the American troops being sent to Europe. Although Pershing aimed to maintain the independence of the AEF, his willingness to integrate into Allied operations helped bring about the Armistice with Germany. After the war, Pershing served as army chief of staff from 1921 to 1924. Born on 13 September 1860 in Laclede, Missouri, he died on 15 July 1948 in Washington, DC. He is buried in Arlington National Cemetery, Virginia. (Robert Cowley and Geoffrey Parker (eds), *The Reader's Companion to Military History*, p. 360.)

5 Alfred von Tirpitz (1849–1930) was chiefly responsible, with the significant support of Kaiser Wilhelm II, for the build-up in strength of the German Navy, including its submarine fleet, from 1897 until the years immediately prior to the First World War. By the time war was declared in the summer of 1914, Germany was able to muster twenty-nine battleships ready for service against the British total of forty-nine. Given such figures, the German fleet would patently not have been able to effectively challenge the British fleet in open action. Tirpitz was promoted to Grand Admiral in 1911 and then Commander of the German Navy with the outbreak of war in 1914. In spite of the high level of support he personally received from Wilhelm II, Tirpitz, aware that the British were well ahead in terms of sea power, remained pessimistic regarding the likely result of any clash between the two great powers. He consequently placed greater emphasis upon a policy of unrestricted submarine construction, preferring to deplete the British fleet piecemeal and by stealth, with the ultimate intention of placing both fleets on a more equal footing. However, the German policy of unrestricted submarine warfare proved highly controversial, most notably with the then neutral USA. Finding his policy thus constrained, Tirpitz tendered his resignation in March 1916, which, somewhat to his surprise, was accepted by Wilhelm II. Born on 19 March 1849 in Küstrin, Germany, he died on 6 March 1930 in Schäftlarn, Germany. He is buried in Munich Waldfriedhof, Munich, Germany. (http://www.firstworldwar.com/bio/tirpitz.htm.)

6   Wilhelm II, or William II, was the last German Emperor and King of Prussia, ruling the German Empire and the Kingdom of Prussia from 15 June 1888 to 9 November 1918. He was one of the most recognisable public figures of the First World War (1914–18). He gained a reputation as a swaggering militarist through his speeches and ill-advised newspaper interviews. While Wilhelm did not actively seek war and tried to hold back his generals from mobilising the German Army in the summer of 1914, his verbal outbursts and his open enjoyment of the title of Supreme War Lord helped bolster the case of those who blamed him for the conflict. His role in the war and his level of responsibility for its outbreak are still controversial. Some historians maintain that Wilhelm was controlled by his generals, while others argue that he retained considerable political power. In late 1918, he was forced to abdicate. He spent the rest of his life in exile in the Netherlands, where he died at the age of 82. Born on 27 January 1859 in Kronprinzenpalais, Berlin, Germany, he died on 4 June 1941 in Huis Doorn, Netherlands.

7   'Freedom of the seas' was the early-twentieth-century idea that the world's oceans served as a global commons for carrying cargo and facilitating commerce. As both communal property and a throughway, the seas could not be controlled by any belligerent power outside of territorial waters, according to the freedom of the seas. (James Leroy Young Jr, 'Freedom of the Seas in 1914–1918', *International Encyclopaedia of the First World War*.)

8   Edward Mandell House (1858–1938), self-styled 'Colonel' House ('Colonel' in nickname only) served as President Woodrow Wilson's closest confidant during the four years of the First World War. Born on 26 July 1858 in Houston, Texas, he died on 28 March 1938 in New York City. (http://www.firstworldwar.com/bio/house.htm.)

9   Field-Marshall Paul Von Hindenburg (1847–1934) was a German military commander during the First World War and later became a German president. He fought in the Austro-Prussian War and in the Franco-German War, and retired as a general in 1911. Recalled to duty at the start of the First World War, Hindenburg shared power with Erich Ludendorff as commander of the Eighth Army and then as chief of the general staff. A national hero for his early victories, Hindenburg later drew the United States into battle with his use of submarine

NOTES

warfare. After retiring again in 1919, he became president of the Weimar Republic in 1925 and died shortly after naming Adolf Hitler the German chancellor. Born 2 October 1847 in Posen, Prussia, he died on 2 August 1934 in Ogrodzieniec, Poland. (Robert Cowley and Geoffrey Parker (eds), *The Reader's Companion to Military History*, Houghton Mifflin Harcourt Publishing Company, 1996, pp. 203–04.)

10 General Erich Ludendorff (1865–1937) was a top German military commander in the latter stages of the First World War. Educated in the cadet corps, Ludendorff was named chief of staff of the Eighth Army after the outbreak of war and earned renown for the victory at the Battle of Tannenberg. He became the nominal deputy to chief of the general staff Paul von Hindenburg and overhauled the army's tactical doctrines, but resigned in October 1918 after the failure of the Ludendorff Offensive. In his later years, he served in Parliament as a member of the National Socialist Party and wrote *Der Totale Krieg (The Nation at War)*. Born on 9 April 1865 in Prussia, he died on 20 December 1938 in Munich, Germany. (Robert Cowley and Geoffrey Parker (eds), *The Reader's Companion to Military History*, Houghton Mifflin Harcourt Publishing Company, 1996, pp. 272–74.)

11 Celestine Murphy (ed.), *Wexford Connections, The Redmond Family and National Politics*, Wexford County Council Public Library Service, September 2014.

12 Dermot Meleady, *John Redmond: The National Leader*, Dublin: Merrion Press, 2014. p. 307.

Chapter 2

1 Born in Weilheim in Oberbayern, Bavaria, on 13 September 1863, Franz Hipper was the son of shopkeeper Anton Hipper and his wife Anna. Having lost his father at age 3, Hipper commenced his education in Munich in 1868 before moving to a gymnasium five years later. He completed his education in 1879 and entered the military as a volunteer officer. Later in the year, Hipper elected to pursue a career in the Kaiserliche Marine and travelled to Kiel. He

passed the required exams and began his training. He was made a probationary sea cadet on 12 April 1881 and spent the summer on the frigate SMS *Niobe*. He returned to the Naval Cadet School in September and he graduated in March 1882. After attending gunnery school, Hipper commenced training at sea. He spent time aboard the training ship SMS *Friedrich Carl* and conducted a world cruise aboard SMS *Leipzig*. In 1918, he succeeded Admiral Reinhard Scheer as commander of the High Seas Fleet. He died on 25 May 1932. (http://www.bbc.co.uk/timelines/zp9x39.)

2   Sir John Rushworth Jellicoe (1859–1935) was Britain's best-known admiral at the start of the war. Born on 5 December 1859 in Southampton, he joined the Royal Navy in 1872 and served in the Egyptian War of 1882. In the years prior to the war, Jellicoe served as Director of Naval Ordnance from 1905–07 and Controller of the Navy from 1908–10. Churchill, then First Lord of the Admiralty, appointed Jellicoe second-in-command of the Grand Fleet in November 1911. He died on 20 November 1935 and is buried in the crypt at St Paul's Cathedral in London. (http://www.firstworldwar.com/bio/jellicoe.htm.)

3   Reinhard Scheer was the admiral who commanded the German High Seas Fleet at the Battle of Jutland (1916). Scheer entered the German Navy in 1879 and by 1907 had become the captain of a battleship. He became chief of staff of the High Seas Fleet under Henning von Holtzendorff in 1910 and commander of a battle squadron in 1913. After the outbreak of the First World War, he advocated for the use of submarines and gained fame as a submarine strategist. He planned subsurface raids off the English coast, using surface units as bait, with submarines lying in ambush for any British ships lured into the open sea. Scheer received command of the fleet in January 1916. He hoped to precipitate a strategic division of the British Grand Fleet and catch it at a disadvantage. A combination of both planning and chance resulted in the two fleets converging at the Battle of Jutland (31 May–1 June 1916), the only major fleet action of the First World War. Although the Grand Fleet was not successfully divided and the British outnumbered the Germans, Scheer's manoeuvring ultimately saved the High Seas Fleet. The battle itself proved indecisive. On 8 August 1918, Scheer succeeded Holtzendorff as chief of the

NOTES

admiralty staff, serving for five months until his retirement. Scheer was born on 30 September 1863 in Obernkirchen, Hanover, Germany, and he died on 26 November 1928 in Marktredwitz, Germany. (www.britannica.com/biography/Reinhard-Sheer.)

4   Robert Cowley and Geoffrey Parker (eds), 'The Battle of Jutland', *The Reader's Companion to Military History*, New York, 1996, pp. 238–39.

5   Nicholas Furlong and John Hayes, *County Wexford in the Rare Oul' Times 1910–1924*, Vol. IV, Wexford, 2005, p. 81.

6   Walther Schwieger (b. 7 April 1885, Berlin, d. 5 September 1917, North Sea) was an officer of the Imperial German Navy (Kaiserliche Marine) and a U-boat commander during the First World War. In 1903 he joined the Imperial German Navy and from 1911 he served with the U-boat service. In 1912 he took command of the U-14 and after the outbreak of war in 1914 he was promoted to Kapitänleutnant and given command of the U-20. Following Schwieger's torpedoing of the RMS *Lusitania*, the United States entered the war. He also was responsible for torpedoing RMS *Hesperian*, a cargo ship which was carrying 800 passengers and also served as a hospital ship, and the SS *Cymbric* on 8 May 1916. Following the scuttling of the U-20, Captain Schwieger took command of U-88. Schwieger was killed in action when his U-boat was chased by HMS *Stonecrop* and the submarine hit a British mine and sank on 5 September 1917, north of Terschelling. During his command of three submarines on thirty-four missions, Captain Schwieger had sunk forty-nine ships, with 183,883 gross register tons. He was the sixth most successful submarine commander of the First World War. He remains entombed in his U-88.

7   Report from the *Free Press* of the loss of the *Leinster* and its victims. This report in the Wexford newspaper brought a local sense of loss to the County Wexford community and highlighted the fatalities caused by the war even at sea. Wexford had suffered the loss of many young men listed among the fallen in France and Belgium.

Chapter 3

1. Joseph Knefler Taussig was born on 30 August 1877 of American parentage in Dresden, Germany, where his father, who also became a Rear Admiral in the navy, was stationed. His father was Edward David Taussig, a native of St Louis, Missouri, and his mother, Ellen Knefler Taussig, was a native of Louisville, Kentucky. Joseph graduated from high school in Washington, DC, in 1895 and was appointed to the Naval Academy that same year. In 1900, whilst a midshipman – a member of the naval forces – Joseph was sent to China with other members to quash a violent anti-foreign and anti-Christian uprising that took place in China between 1899 and 1901. Near Tientsin, Joseph was wounded and sent to a hospital to recover with an English captain, John Jellicoe, who was chief of staff for Admiral Seymour, who was in charge of the British forces. It was a legend of sorts that grew up around Joseph that diplomatic relations were not something new to him. In addition, a letter from Admiral Jellicoe was handed to Joseph in Queenstown in May 1917, welcoming him and the American Navy to the battle zone. Having achieved the rank of Vice-Admiral, Joseph Taussig died on 29 October 1947 in Bethesda, Maryland, and is buried at Arlington National Cemetery.
2. Lewis Bayly was born at Woolwich on 28 September 1857. Bayly joined the Royal Navy in 1870. On 22 March 1908, Bayly was appointed a naval aide-de-camp to King Edward VII. He was then given a shore command as president of the Royal Naval War College (1908–11). Before the outbreak of the war, he was given command of the 1st Battlecruiser Squadron (1911–12) and of the 3rd Battle Squadron (1913–14). In 1915 he was made president of the Royal Naval College, Greenwich. In 1916 he was made Senior Officer on the Coast of Ireland (later the title became Commander-in-Chief, Coast of Ireland). He held this post at Queenstown from 1915 until 1919. In this role, Bayly was tasked with keeping the approaches to Britain safe from U-boat attacks. In 1917, Bayly, promoted to admiral, was given command of a mixed British-American force defending the Western Approaches. He took as his chief of staff the American captain Joel R.P. Pringle. Bayly had a good working relationship with his US

NOTES

counterpart William Sims. Admiral Bayly retired in 1919. He died in London in 1938. (http://www.nationalpubliclibrary.org.)

3   Q-ships were introduced towards the close of 1914 by the British and French – and later deployed by the Italian and Russians navies. Q-ships were deployed as an anti-submarine weapon. Alternatively referred to as Special Service Ships or Mystery Ships, the purpose of Q-ships was straightforward: to trap enemy (usually German) submarines. Invariably comprised of small freighters or old trawlers, they were loaded with hidden guns in a collapsible deck structure. In practice, U-boats would hail Q-ships flying (in the case of the Royal Navy) the merchant red ensign and, in the period before the implementation of Germany's policy of unrestricted submarine warfare in 1917, a so-called 'panic party' would apparently abandon the Q-ship prior to the usual German policy of approaching the enemy vessel to sink it with the minimum depletion of ammunition. At this stage, the use of torpedoes to sink relatively small vessels was officially frowned upon. Thus, with the U-boat effectively lured towards the apparently abandoned vessel, the Q-ship would run up the white ensign and the deck structure would be collapsed by the remaining ship's crew, revealing a series of up to four manned guns, which would immediately open fire. Initially successful, the Q-ship ploy resulted in the sinking of some eleven enemy U-boats by the British and French. As the war progressed, the production of Q-ships increased notably so that by the war's close, the British alone deployed 366. However the Germans quickly developed a certain caution about approaching small enemy vessels, wary of decoys. Torpedoes were increasingly used to sink Q-ships at longer range and, with the introduction of unrestricted submarine warfare, the crews of Q-ships were not given time to abandon ship before being fired upon. The British lost sixty-one Q-ships in total. By 1917 the effectiveness of Q-ship deployment was minimal and the overall endeavour could not be termed a success. (http://www.firstworldwar.com/atoz/qships.htm.)

4   William Sowden Sims (1858–1936), an American admiral, commanded the United States naval forces in European waters during the First World War. He was born in Port Hope, Ontario, on 15 October 1858. After graduating from the US Naval Academy in

1880, he served in the Atlantic (1880–88) and the Pacific (1889–97). He was American naval attaché in Paris during the Spanish–American War. After additional service as attaché in St Petersburg, Russia and further duty at sea, he became inspector of target practice for the US Asiatic fleet. He first came to public notice when he argued vigorously that gunnery was ineffective and in need of modernisation. President Theodore Roosevelt made him his naval aide (1907–09).

5   Pat Fitzgerald, *Down Paths of Gold: A Portrait of Cork Harbour's Southern Shore*, Cork: Litho Press Co. 1992. pp. 14–25.
6   http://www.centenialofflight.gov/essay/Aerospace/Curtiss/Aero2.htm.
7   http://www.militaryfactory.com.
8   Pat Fitzgerald, *Down Paths of Gold: A Portrait of Cork Harbour's Southern Shore*, Litho Press Co. Cork, 1992. pp. 14–25.

Chapter 4

1   In August 1914, the Royal Navy Air Service Station (RNAS) opened at Killingholme, later to pass in 1918 to American control during the First World War, when it housed over forty seaplanes. The US Navy flew their Curtiss flying boats from the seaplane base, continuing with North Sea patrols to the end of the war, when the station was returned to British control. The base was closed in 1920. One of the launching slipways survived until 1920, when it was demolished for safety reasons. (http://www.abandonedairfields.co.uk/united-kingdom/england/killingholme-s 1029.)
2   In the early part of 1918, the United States decided to set up a naval aviation force with the objective of destroying the enemy submarine bases in Belgium. The method of destruction was to be continuous day and night bombing. The bombing force would be made up of marine and naval squadrons and would be known as the Northern Bombing Group. The location chosen for the supply base was Eastleigh where the British Air Ministry were offering the use of an Aircraft Acceptance Park on the site that would in later years become Southampton/Eastleigh Airport. An inspection of the site on 4 July 1918 revealed that the construction of hangars and other buildings

NOTES

was well underway and the decision was made to accept the offer. The US Navy formally took command on 20 July under Lt Gen. DeC. Chevalier, who on 26 October 1922 would be the first ever pilot to land on the US's new aircraft carrier, the USS *Langley*. The base became known as Base B. After the end of hostilities, the rundown of facilities was very rapid and on 10 April 1919 Eastleigh reverted to British command. The RAF occupied the base until January 1920, at which time it was closed, remaining officially out of use until it was reopened as an airport in November 1932. (Courtesy of Dave Fagan, Torquay, England.)

3   See Chapter 8, 'Wexford 1918', for an account of both events.
4   Taken from copies of diary entries made by Chief Petty Officer John J. O'Brien while serving at the USN Air Station, Ferrybank, Wexford, in 1918 during the First World War. Facsimiles of the diaries were given by his wife, Irene O'Brien, Philadelphia, USA, following a visit to Wexford in 1977, to one of Wexford's most prominent walking tour guides, former Sergeant Major Walter Doyle. Mr Doyle, being aware of the importance of such documents, made them available to Nicholas Furlong, historian, author and correspondent for *The People* newspaper group, who noted and quoted from the diaries in his Pat O'Leary weekly column in *The People* newspaper. Fridays, 15 and 29 December 1978, p. 28, p. 10 and Friday, 5 January, 1979, p. 5.
5   Ibid.
6   Ibid.
7   Ibid.
8   The Marquis of Ely, Charles Lord Viscount Loftus, Mayor of Wexford, 1793. The house named after the marquis was built in 1817 by Robert Hughes. His son, Robert Wygram Hughes, inherited the house and in turn Robert's sister Georgina inherited it in 1859. She married a Doran. The property went down to her son, later to become General Sir John Doran. He lived at Ely House until his death in 1903. His widow lived there until her death in 1912. The house was taken over during the First World War by the British Admiralty under the Defence of the Realm Act (DORA) and the property was also used as an American Air Base in 1918–19. The son of General Doran, Major General Doran, lived in the house from 1919 to 1943. The entire property was sold to the order of St John of God and served

as a hospital. It expanded to become a modern hospital in 1975, by which time the original house had been demolished. (David Rowe and Eithne Scallan, *Some Houses of Wexford*, Ballinakilla, 2004, House No. 460.)

9 Bann-a-boo House was probably part of the Ely House estate and the house was possibly built around the same time as Ely House (1817, by Robert Hughes). At the time it was described as a cottage comprising seven bedrooms, an elegant drawing room, a study, a dining room overlooking the yard, a kitchen, a scullery and a glassed-in porch giving a beautiful view across the river at night. The Doran family leased the property to the Millers of Rathmacknee and also to Colonel John R. McGrath, owner of registered motor car MI 1. The property then went on to Miss Madalena Spring, who was joined by her brother, Captain Richard Spring, on the death of his wife. (David Rowe and Eithne Scallan, *Some Houses of Wexford*, Ballinakilla, 2004, House No. 206.)

10 Pat O'Leary column detailing information submitted by Bill Cronin, newspaper man, writer and former editor of Wexford's second local newspaper, *The Free Press*. Friday, 29 December 1978, p. 10.

11 O'Brien diaries, entry for 5 April 1918.

12 O'Brien diaries. Daily roster as outlined by Commander Herbster: revelry – 5 a.m.; coffee at 5.15; turn-to at 5.30; knock-off 6.45 a.m. for breakfast at 7 a.m. Turn-to again at 7.30; knock-off at 11.45; turn-to again at 12.30 p.m.; knock-off at 5.45 p.m.; chow at 6 p.m.; turn-to – 6.30p.m.; knock-off at 9 p.m. Stand watch midnight to 4 a.m. to 8 a.m.

13 Joseph A. Fabula, seaman

14 Thomas R. Allfrey, Chief Carpenter's Mate.

15 Samuel Lanford, known as 'The Boston Tar Baby' also 'The Boston Bonecrusher' (1883–1956).

16 John L. Sullivan (1858–1918), first heavyweight champion of gloved boxing. Born in Boston of Irish parents. Was known as 'The Boston Strong Boy'.

17 Harry A. Mazzie, Machinist's Mate Second Class.

18 Willie Ritchie born Gerhardt Anthony Steffen in San Francisco in 1891. His boxing career began in 1907. He became lightweight champion when he defeated Ad Wolgast in November 1912. He died in 1975.

NOTES

19 Lieut. (jg) C.B. Tillotson, assisted by C.E. Riley and G.E. James (ed. and comp.), US Naval Air Station, Wexford, Souvenir Booklet.
20 O'Brien diaries, entry for 2 September 1918.
21 Ibid.
22 Glossary of terms used in the letter: 'juice' = electrical power; 'brig' = a US term for a naval military prison or a jail on a ship; 'eats' = food; 'galley' = ship's kitchen.
23 Lieut. (jg) C.B. Tillotson, assisted by C.E. Riley and G.E. James (ed. and comp.), US Naval Air Station, Wexford, Souvenir Booklet.
24 Ibid.
25 Ibid.

Chapter 5

1 A.B. Feuer, *The U.S. Navy in World War I: Combat at Sea and in the Air*, USA, 1999, p. 129.
2 Ibid.
3 The float is a slender pontoon mounted under the fuselage to provide buoyancy to the aircraft.
4 The Ballast Bank was built in 1831 to permit boats leaving port without cargo to take on ballast of rocks or sand for stability. Also ships arriving in ballast could deposit their ballast at the Ballast Bank and the vessel would be ready for loading its cargo at the quayside. (Rossiter, Roche, Hurley, Hayes, *Walk Wexford Ways*, Wexford, 1988, p. 27.)
5 Onion skin paper is a very smooth, lightweight, translucent paper containing a high percentage of cotton fibres. Mainly used in airmail stationery, origami and other paper crafts. (www.the papermillstore.com.)
6 Diary entry by Chief Petty Officer John J. O'Brien while serving at the USN Air Station, Ferrybank, Wexford in 1918 during the First World War.
7 Lieut. (jg) C.B. Tillotson, assisted by C.E. Riley and G.E. James (ed. and comp.), US Naval Air Station, Wexford, Souvenir Booklet.
8 A.B. Feuer, *The U.S. Navy in World War I: Combat at Sea and in the Air*, USA, 1999, p. 121.
9 Ibid, p. 123.

10 Brogans were heavy, ankle-high shoes or boots and were standard issue for aviators.

Chapter 7

1. The co-ordinates for Rosslare Harbour are 52.2513°N, 6.3415°W.
2. The co-ordinates for Fishguard are 51.9938°N, 4.9763°W.
3. Gerry Breen (ed.), *Rosslare in History*, Wexford, 2005, pp. 16–17.
4. Ibid.
5. Charles Dodd, one of the two brothers brought over to operate the station by Marconi, married Kathleen Kelly, eldest daughter of William J. and Mary Kelly, founders of Kelly's Resort Hotel at Rosslare. (Bill and Vonnie Kelly, with Ronan Foster, *The Book of Kelly's*, Dublin, 1995, pp. 17–18.)
6. Ibid.
7. Italian-born Guglielmo Marconi had strong Co. Wexford connections. Marconi was born at Palazzo Dall'Armi Marescalchi, Bologna, on 25 April 1874. His mother was Annie Jameson of Daphne Castle, Enniscorthy, and a daughter of the Jameson family of distillers. Guglielmo Marconi, 1st Marquis of Marconi, inventor and electrical engineer, was known for his pioneering work on long-distance radio transmission and for his development of Marconi's law and a radio telegraph system. He died on 20 July 1937 in Rome. Gerry Breen (ed.), *Rosslare in History*, Wexford, 2005, pp. 16–17.
8. Four Winds still stands today and serves as a holiday residence for the Presentation Sisters owners of the property. (Oral interview with Sr. Grace Redmond, Presentation Sisters, Wexford.)
9. The co-ordinates for Greenore Point are; 52.2383°N, 6.3069°W.
10. Sir William Joshua Goulding, 1st Baronet (1856–1925) of the Goulding Baronetcy of Millicent in Clane, Co. Kildare and Roebuck Hill, Dundrum. This title was created on 22 August 1904 for the businessman William Goulding, a prominent freemason and director of several railway companies in Ireland. He was son of William Goulding (1817–84), the last Conservative MP for Cork City. (http://www.discovery.nationalarchives.gov.uk.)
11. Roy Stokes, *U-Boat Alley*, Gorey, Co. Wexford: Compuwreck, 2004, p. 111.

NOTES

12 Ibid.
13 A naval drifter is a boat built along the lines of a commercial fishing drifter but fitted out for naval purposes.
14 John Maddock, *Rosslare Harbour – past and present*, Harbour Publications, 1986, pp. 53–54.
15 Ibid.
16 Ibid.
17 Ibid.
18 Roy Stokes, *U-Boat Alley*, Gorey, Co. Wexford: Compuwreck, 2004, pp. 112–13.
19 Ibid.
20 Ibid.
21 The co-ordinates for Tuskar Rock Lighthouse are 52.12175°N, 6.12445°W.
22 John Maddock, *Rosslare Harbour – past and present*, Harbour Publications, 1986, p. 105.
23 Gerry Breen (ed.), *Rosslare in History*, Wexford, 2005, pp. 16–17.
24 John Maddock, *Rosslare Harbour – past and present*, Harbour Publications, 1986, p. 55.
25 Gerry Breen (ed.), *Rosslare in History*, Wexford, 2005, pp.16–17.
26 List of names of lighthouse keepers courtesy of Mr Frank Pelly.
27 Roy Stokes, *U-Boat Alley*, Gorey, Co. Wexford: Compuwreck, 2004, p. 118.

Chapter 8

1 The author has edited the newspaper reports to make for a more concise account of the event or news item.
2 *The People*, Thursday, 31 January 1918.
3 *The People*, Saturday, 27 January, 1918.
4 *The Free Press*, Saturday, 9 February 1918, p. 8.
5 *The Free Press*, Saturday, 16 February 1918.
6 *The Free Press*, Saturday, 23 February 1918.
7 *The Free Press*, Tuesday, 9 March 1918, p. 4.
8 Photograph published in souvenir booklet, *In Memoriam Major Willie Redmond*, Dublin, 1918, 2nd edition.

9   *The Free Press*, Saturday, 2 March 1918, p. 8.
10 *The Free Press*, Saturday, 9 March 1918, p. 9.
11 *The Free Press*, Saturday, 11 May 1918, p. 3.
12 Wexford Borough Council Minute Books 1918-19, Vol. 7, Minutes, Part 1, Nov. 1917–Dec. 1921, p. 36.
13 *The Free Press*, Saturday, 20 July 1918, p. 6.
14 *The Free Press*, Saturday, 24 August 1918, p. 8.
15 *The Free Press*, Saturday, 21 September 1918, p. 7.
16 *The Free Press*, Saturday, 9 November 1918, p. 8.
17 *The Free Press*, Saturday, 30 November 1918, p. 8.
18 *The Free Press*, 1918, p. 4.
19 Fr Patrick Kavanagh (1834–1916), was born in Wexford on North Main Street. A Franciscan friar, he was educated in Wexford and Rome. He was a grand-nephew of Fr Michael Murphy, the fighting priest of 1798. Fr Kavanagh wrote *A Popular History of the Insurrection of 1798*. He unveiled the bronze statue by sculptor Oliver Sheppard of the Pikeman in Wexford's Bull Ring on Sunday, 6 August 1905. (Liam Gaul, *A Window on the Past*, 2012, p. 24.)

Chapter 9

1   Admiral Sir David Beatty (1871–1936), of Borodale House, Bree, County Wexford, is regarded as one of Britain's naval heroes. David joined the navy as a young man and graduated through the ranks. At the battles of Scapa Flow (1914) and Jutland (1916), Beatty served with distinction. On his retirement he held the rank of Admiral of the Fleet. He was created Viscount Borodale. His brother, Major Charles Beatty (1870–1917) lived at Borodale, where he worked the estate after their father's death in 1904. Admiral Sir David Beatty returned periodically on family visits and for hunting holidays in the Bree district but never intended to return permanently to live at Borodale. Following Major Charles Beatty's death due to an aggravated war wound in 1917, the estate was administered by the Beattys' stepmother, Mrs Anita Lett. Due to mismanagement of the estate and accumulating debts, there was nothing left by the time Major Beatty's son, Charles, was set to take over the estate. The Irish Land Commission disposed of the lands

NOTES

in around 1937. Borodale House was dismantled and plundered until it disappeared from the landscape. (Dan Walsh, *100 Wexford Country Houses, an illustrated history*, Enniscorthy, 1996, p. 21.)

2   Seamus and Joe Seery, 'World War I – The Wexford Casualties', *Journal of the Taghmon Historical Society*, No. 3, Taghmon, 1999, pp. 54–96.

Chapter 10

1   A personal interview with Mr Charles Delaney, nephew of Elizabeth (Delaney) Phillips. Mr Delaney formerly resided with his parents at the Delaney family home at Francis Street, Wexford. During my interview Charles Delaney generously gave me access to many photographs pertaining to the USN Air Station at Ferrybank, Wexford, during the First World War. Many of these photographs are reproduced in this book.

2   McNichol makes a reference to several people in the opening section of this letter, namely to a Leander and a Joe, both of whom seem to have also been in the US Forces serving overseas. He also refers to a person named Gert, who was Bill Toomey's sister Gertrude, as noted in a letter written to her from Liverpool on Saturday, 2 June 1919. The letter was addressed to 'Miss Gertrude Toomey, Beacon St. Arlington, Mass.'

3   The nearest beach to Ferrybank would have been Curracloe, renowned for its fine, almost white, soft sandy beach and safe swimming. It is still a popular beach and attracts many visitors. Part of *Saving Private Ryan* was filmed on the beach.

4   Reference to the 'Fourth' was obviously a reference to Independence Day on 4 July.

5   Edenvale and the Sow River – the waterfall at Edenvale, although in the parish of Crossabeg, is caused by the presence of a mass of hard rock across the Sow River. The hardness of the rock was a result of it being subjected to heat as well as pressure. The surrounding local rock was subjected to pressure only and so it is softer and eroded more easily, leaving the hard rock to form a barrier. (Dr Edward Culleton, 'The Landscape of Castlebridge', in Rev. Walter Forde (ed.), *The Castlebridge Story*, Kara Publications, 2009. p. 9.)

6   The town hall is situated in the Cornmarket, Wexford town. It was built in 1775 as a market house and the lower windows were formerly arched recesses for the traders. Inside there was a magnificent ballroom and supper room. Today the building serves as Wexford Arts Centre. (Rossiter, Roche, Hurley, Hayes, *Walk Wexford Ways*, Wexford, 1988, p. 56.)

7   Personal interview with Eddie Macken. The premises at No. 63 North Main Street, Wexford, was the 'Cape of Good Hope', a public house frequented by Wexford businessmen and mariners, hence the title. This premises was the home of the Thirteen Club. Members of this club had to consume thirteen glasses of whiskey punch in quick succession to be deemed a member. The proprietor at that time was Mr J.P. Keating. This public house still trades as 'The Cape', a shortened version of its original title and has been in the ownership of the Macken family for over seventy-five years.

8   Founded by William and Mary Kelly in 1895 as Kelly's Tea Rooms, it quickly developed into a hotel. At one time, the hotel was also the local post office. William's wife, Mary, was postmistress of Rosslare when the tearooms first opened. Nicholas Kelly, son of the founder, took over the running of the hotel in the mid-1920s. Nicholas and his wife Kathleen had three children, Patsy, Billy and Christine. It was their son, Billy, who took over the hotel and developed the business as Kelly's Resort Hotel. The fourth generation of the Kelly family, Bill and his wife Isabelle are now in charge of this very successful hotel. (Bill and Vonnie Kelly, with Ronan Foster, *The Book of Kelly's*.)

Chapter 11

1   Three Supermarine Walrus Is were purchased for the Irish Army Air Corps in 1939, which had been diverted from a batch of 160 (L2169-L2336), constructed by Supermarine Aviation Works (Vickers) Ltd, for the Fleet Air Arm. Supermarine Class B marks N18, N19 and N20 were allotted by the company to the three flying boats and were retained as serial numbers while in service with the Air Corps. 15 Serial No.: N18. Construction No.: 6S/21840. Previous Identity: L2301. First flight: 24.2.39. Did not enter service with the Fleet Air

NOTES

Arm. Service History: Force-landed during delivery flight, due to engine failure, near Ballytrent, Co. Wexford, 3.3.39. Upper wing structure damaged and transported by road to Baldonnell Aerodrome for repairs. Did not enter service until 1941 when wings from another Walrus I (N19) were fitted. To No. 1 Coastal Patrol Squadron. To General Purpose Flight, 1944. 'Withdrawn from use', 8.8.45. To Aer Lingus Teo., EI-ACC. Purchased for No. 615 Squadron, R. Auxiliary A.F., March 1947. G-AIZG. Sold for scrap, 1949. Restored for static display at Fleet Air Arm Museum, Yeovilton, 1963–66. Serial No.: N19. Construction No.: Not known. Previous Identity: L2302. First flight, 10.1.39. Did not enter service with the Fleet Air Arm. Service History: Delivered to Baldonnell Aerodrome, 4.3.39. To No. 1 Coastal Patrol Squadron. (Patrick J. Cummins, *Aircraft of the Irish Air Service, Irish Army Air Corps and Irish Air Corps, 1922–2007*, May 2007, with permission granted by Mrs. Maura Cummins, Waterford.)

2 The Rosslare Harbour Lifeboat, the *KECF*, was a 45ft 6in twin-engine cabin class Watson motor lifeboat. She was fitted with a short-range wireless so her crew could maintain contact with the lifeboat station at Rosslare Harbour. This lifeboat began her service at Rosslare Harbour in April 1927 and served until March 1939, having carried out sixty-three launches and saving 127 lives. Her escorting of the Irish Air Force seaplane to safety was her final mission on 6 March 1939. The *KECF* was sold out of service in December 1956. (Nicholas Leach, *The Lifeboats of Rosslare Harbour and Wexford*, pp. 59, 67, 137, 156.)

3 *The People*, Wednesday, 8 March 1939.

4 Nicky Rossiter, 'Sixty Five Years Ago in Castlebridge', *The Bridge Magazine*, Vol. 8, No. 2, 2004, p. 24.

5 **Technical Details – Role** - Spotter reconnaissance amphibian with crew of three. **Manufacturers** - Vickers Supermarine **Power plant** - One 775hp Bristol Pegasus II, M2 or VI. **Wingspan** - 45ft 10ins. **Length** - 37ft 3ins. **Height** - 15ft 3ins. **Weight** - 8,050lbs loaded. **Max speed** - 135mph at 4,750ft. **Range** - 444 nautical miles. **Armament** - One Vickers K in bow and either one or two Vickers K guns amidships, both cockpits with Scarff rings, provision for six 100lb or two 250lb bombs or two MkVIII depth charges below the wings.

6   Anti-fouling paints are used to coat the bottoms of ships to prevent sea life such as algae and molluscs attaching themselves to the hull, thereby slowing down the ship and increasing fuel consumption. The new convention defines 'anti-fouling systems' as 'a coating, paint, surface treatment, surface or device that is used on a ship to control or prevent attachment of unwanted organisms'. (http://www.imo.org/anti-fouling systems.)

If you enjoyed this book, you may also be interested in…

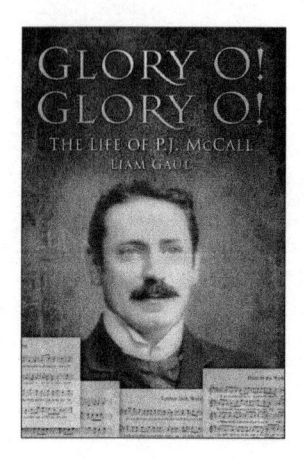

Glory O! Glory O!
LIAM GAUL

Patrick Joseph McCall (1861-1919) was a musician best remembered for his epic ballad of the Insurrection of 1798, 'Boolavogue'. His ballads stand as the soundtrack for much of the history of the area, and his life, both in music and through his efforts to change the lives of Dublin's poor, stands as a monument to a man dedicated to others. In this volume, Liam Gaul, author of several previous books on Irish music history, records the life and work of P.J. McCall, artist and poet, and his influence on the Irish musical tradition.

9781845886950

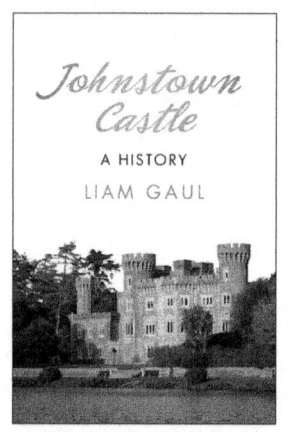

Johnstown Castle: A History
LIAM GAUL

The harmony between great castles and their ornamental grounds is rarely seen in such perfect form as at Johnstown Castle. The gardens and grounds were designed by Daniel Robertson, of Powerscourt fame, assisted by Martin Day. The castle itself was home to two prominent Wexford families, the Esmondes and the Grogans, who have between them occupied the grounds from the fifteenth century right up to 1945. This book is the first published history of the castle, and in these pages author, historian and Wexford native Liam Gaul, explores the development of this imposing aspect of Wexford and national heritage from its earliest beginnings.

9781845888268

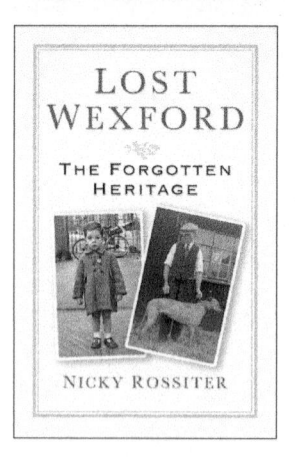

Lost Wexford
NICKY ROSSITER

Over the years trades, streets, buildings, shops and a myriad of other items have gone from Wexford's landscape. However, this book recalls not only these physical losses but also includes the many items of culture, local lore and other ephemeral heritage that disappears by the week. With chapters on industry, religious practices, entertainment and Wexford characters, this fascinating compendium this can be dipped into time and time again to reveal something new about the people, the heritage and the secrets of this maritime town.

9781845885885

Visit our websites and discover thousands of other History Press books.

www.thehistorypress.ie
www.thehistorypress.co.uk

The History Press Ireland